New Woman Writers, Authority and the Body

New Woman Writers, Authority and the Body

Edited by

Melissa Purdue and Stacey Floyd

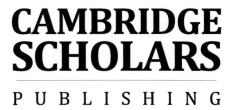

New Woman Writers, Authority and the Body, Edited by Melissa Purdue and Stacey Floyd

This book first published 2009

Cambridge Scholars Publishing

12 Back Chapman Street, Newcastle upon Tyne, NE6 2XX, UK

British Library Cataloguing in Publication Data
A catalogue record for this book is available from the British Library

ISBN (10): 1-4438-0613-7, ISBN (13): 978-1-4438-0613-8

TABLE OF CONTENTS

ACKNOWLEDGEMENTS

Versions of the essays in this collection were originally presented at the 18th and 19th-Century British Women Writers Conference held in Lexington, Kentucky in April of 2007. We would like to thank the conference presenters, attendees, keynote speakers and our fellow co-organizers: Katherine Osborne, Hannah Freeman and Christopher Reese. Thank you also to Ellen Bayuk Rosenman for her support of the conference and her encouragement to us.

INTRODUCTION

. . . power, to put it plainly, was what the modern woman craved.
—Ella Hepworth Dixon, *The Story of a Modern Woman*

With the Married Woman's Property Act in 1882, the repeal of the Contagious Disease Acts in 1886, and an 1891 act that denied men conjugal rights to the wives' bodies without their wives' consent,[1] late-nineteenth-century women (upper and middle-class white women in particular) were granted more rights and began to envision new possibilities for themselves. In particular, "New Women" began writing about their desire for increased women's rights.[2] These New Woman writers of the *fin de siècle* created a distinctly different body of literature that reflected their concerns about women's limited role in society. Although New Woman writers did not always agree on solutions to the problems that faced them, their texts did engage with common themes like marriage reform, social activism, motherhood, equality in education, sexual freedom and greater career opportunities.

New Woman texts also often offer new and progressive portrayals of women's authority as connected to strong physical bodies. In Sarah Grand's *The Beth Book*, the heroine discovers that she is married to a despicable man who is unfaithful, who works as a doctor at a Lock Hospital and who practices vivisection on innocent animals without a second thought. His combined disregard for her body, along with those of the women he treats for suspected venereal disease and the animals he tortures, is simply too much for Beth. She leaves to start a different life on her terms. Beth, like many other heroines in novels by New Woman authors, claims her body as her own and fights for the rights of others. The body is, in fact, of central importance in the New Woman's struggle for women's rights. It is one of the main sites of resistance as well as one of the first to be commented upon by critics. New Woman writers "author" their own bodies by acknowledging women's sexual desires;

---

[1] Sally Ledger, *The New Woman*, p.11.
[2] Sarah Grand (Frances Elizabeth Clarke McFall) first used the tern "New Woman" in her 1894 article "The New Aspect of the Woman Question," published in the *North American Review*.

advocating rational dress for increased mobility; challenging the expectation that all women must want to become mothers; and by emphasizing the importance of healthy, active bodies and real appetites in girls. Essentially, they create a new identity for themselves through the construction of this new female body—one that projects power and freedom. It is this centrality of the body and quest for authority that the essays in this collection address.

As was evidenced by the large number of presentations on New Woman authors at the recent 18th & 19th-Century British Women Writers Conference held in Lexington, Kentucky, there is growing interest in the field of New Woman studies.[3] The essays in this collection add to current scholarship, focusing on themes ranging from the New Woman's relationship with Darwinian theory to athletics for women and the New Woman's navigation of urban life. The collection begins with Bryony Randall's exploration of George Egerton's short fiction and the ambiguities and anxieties with which the figure of the literary writer was imbued. Randall looks at the perceived threats to 'authority', narrowly and broadly defined, embodied in the New Woman, focusing on Egerton's "A Lost Masterpiece: A City Mood, Aug. '93." She examines the tension set up between the masculine voice of the narrator and the female figures encountered in the text in the context of an era of "art for art's sake" in which women's paid work was viewed as potentially contaminating the high art of the male establishment.

The collection moves next to Tracy J.R. Collins' essay on *In the House of My Pilgrimage*, an autobiography by Lillian M. Faithfull, in which Collins locates the New Woman's drive for equality in an early engagement in physical fitness, athletics, and sports. Abigail Mann then examines Mona Caird's complicated relationship with Darwinian theory as witnessed in her anti-vivisection pamphlets and *The Daughters of Danaus*. While New Woman scholars have acknowledged Sarah Grand's debts to Darwinian theory, Mann here offers new insight into Caird's own engagement with biological theory. Casey Cothran continues the conversation about Mona Caird by exploring the use of suffering as a tool of social protest in *The Daughters of Danaus*. Cothran argues that Caird's novel can be seen as part of a larger cultural examination of the violence

---

[3] The conference, themed "Speaking With Authority," included sixteen individual papers focusing on New Woman writers in addition to a special roundtable discussion on the New Woman between Teresa Mangum, Sally Mitchell and Ann Ardis.

enacted on women's bodies (by outside forces and by women themselves) in the decades both preceding and following the turn of the century.

The next two essays in the collection focus on the New Woman's relationships with texts and with other women. Donna Decker looks at Charlotte Bronte's *Jane Eyre* and the ways in which the text inspired and informed George Egerton's *The Wheel of God*, examining the importance of reading in New Woman texts—both the reading of words and bodies. Kelly Hulander's insightful essay argues that the success and happiness of female protagonists in New Woman fiction, particularly fiction set in urban environments, depends heavily on the supportive relationships they either maintain or cultivate with other independent women. The collection closes with Tamar Heller's reading of Rhoda Broughton's *A Fool in Her Folly* as a metafictional exploration of the obstacles faced by the female author writing about sexuality before the advent of the New Woman. Heller illuminates Broughton's dissection of the psychological pressures faced by the woman writer who strives—but who, unlike the women of Woolf's generation, cannot yet succeed—in exorcising the Angel in the House.

CHAPTER ONE

GEORGE EGERTON'S "A LOST MASTERPIECE": INSPIRATION, GENDER, AND CULTURAL AUTHORITY AT THE *FIN DE SIÈCLE*

BRYONY RANDALL

George Egerton's short story with the unwieldy title "A Lost Masterpiece: A City Mood, Aug. '93" was published in April of 1894 in the first issue of John Lane's radical and short-lived quarterly *The Yellow Book*.[1] In the second issue, in an article entitled "The Yellow Book criticized", one Philip Gilbert Hamerton LL.D. acknowledges that the story "shows the same qualities of style" as displayed in Egerton's short story collection *Keynotes*, but ultimately dismisses "A Lost Masterpiece" as a failure, judging that "the subject is too unfruitful, merely a literary disappointment, because a bright idea has been chased away" (185). Perhaps subsequent readers have tended to agree with Hamerton–who, it should be noted, was explicitly invited to articulate negative judgments on the first issue by the editors of the *Yellow Book*, as an example of the magazine's intention to "welcom[e] dissent" (Stetz and Lasner, 11). Nevertheless, reactions similar to Hamerton's may in part explain why this short story has received so little critical attention and has not, unlike many of Egerton's other stories, been reprinted since its first appearance. But there are, perhaps, other reasons for its relative neglect even since the resurgence of interest in Egerton's work over the last couple of decades.

Egerton criticism has generally focused on the stories collected in *Keynotes* and *Discords*, published in 1893 and 1894 respectively. Those stories that have a clearly female narrator have been of particular interest, as they tend to enable Egerton to state most vividly the critique of sexual politics that is at the heart of her literary project. And female narrators are in the majority in Egerton's stories (only one of the stories collected in *Keynotes* and *Discords* has an explicitly male narrator); indeed, as Kate McCullough has noted, many of her stories involve a kind of "double" female narrator, using "a narrative structured by one woman's telling of her story to another sympathetic woman", where the sympathetic woman is usually the story's primary narrator (207). By contrast, the gender of the narrator of "A Lost Masterpiece", whose brilliant "literary idea" is "chased away", is never actually stated. The few previous commentators on the story have tended to read the narrator as female–perhaps, even, simply assumed that the narrator is a woman (Stetz 28; Turner 153; Parejo leaves the question open, 23-24)–not surprising given the prevalence of female narrators in Egerton's work. However, I argue that Egerton's text actually invites us to read its narrator as, if not necessarily actually male, at least highly masculinized, and the way in which this masculinized figure articulates the experience of inspiration, as well as the experience of losing a literary idea, presents an intriguing exploration of the gender anxiety around masculine literary authority in the 1890s.

A summary of the story will give an early indication of some of the masculine aspects of the narrator–in particular, his/her depiction as that familiar figure of the *fin-de-siècle*, the *flâneur*. [2] "A Lost Masterpiece" begins with the narrator describing having returned to town from the countryside, responding to a "desire to mix with the crowd, to lay my ear once more to the heart of the world and listen to its life-throbs" (Egerton, "A Lost Masterpiece", 196). The narrator then takes a walk through the city (later shown to be London), but also makes use of the various means of transport available to the late nineteenth-century *flâneur*: he or she takes a short trip on a river steamer, and is laughed at by two young girls, smiles at "a pretty anaemic city girl" (192), observes the crowd with an ironic detachment, and mounts an omnibus. There the narrator's attention is taken by a woman walking along the pavement. All the while an idea for a "literary gem" (196) is being developed: while the narrator's "outer eyes" catch every external detail, his or her "inner eyes" see "undercurrents of beauty and pathos", out of which the idea is formed (190, 191). So far, so Baudelairean; a *flâneur* with literary aspirations becomes inexplicably fascinated by a female *passante*. However, in an uncharacteristically negative turn (uncharacteristic, that is, for depictions of the *flâneur/passante* relationship)[3], it is this woman who, in the narrator's words, "murders fancy" (196)–murders the "delicate creation of my brain, begotten by the fusion of country and town" (195), the idea or inspiration that has been evolving in the narrator's mind since the beginning of the story.

In addition to this depiction of the narrator as *flâneur*, the story features an interaction between the narrator and a woman on the street that figures the narrator as sexual predator. Further, the narrator betrays an undeniably misogynist attitude, using language about the women he or she encounters entirely dissimilar from that used by Egerton's female narrators. These points, amplifying my sense of the narrator as masculine, will be discussed at greater length below. Here, however, we need to address the question of how to read this figure, whom I have been awkwardly designating "her or she".

If we are to follow previous critics in designating the narrator female, we need to find some rationale for "her" masculinized articulations and demeanor. One explanation might be that they form part of her depiction of herself as an inspired writer, and a genius. To be a writer of this sort involves discursive cross-dressing; a woman must speak in a masculine voice to be audible as this kind of writer. We can see how this cross-dressing might have been necessary, and might be ripe for Egerton's critique, if we consider Timothy Clark's argument that inspiration, as it has traditionally been figured, relies on an anticipated audience: "the scene of composition is already a prolepsis of recognition" (29). Clark goes on to observe the implications of this for women writers, namely that "[inspiration] may well not have been available to women for a long time in terms so easily recuperable as a stance of public authority", given that historically a woman may have been "unable to forsee fair recognition or fair reception, [having] few socially sanctioned images of authorship available to her" (33). Egerton is writing at a moment when, crucially, women writers were beginning to see the possibility of fair, or at least fairer, recognition. Similarly, it was part of the feminist movement with which Egerton was, at this time, so emphatically associated, to generate and circulate "images of female authorship" and work towards their being "socially sanctioned". In producing a figure of an inspired writer-to-be, laden with masculine traits–not least among which is the vivid anticipation of a joyful public reception, readers who "would flock to thank me" (Egerton, "A Lost Masterpiece", 194)–but whose gender is not made clear, and who thus may be a woman, Egerton seems deliberately to be drawing attention to the gendering of "socially sanctioned images" of authorship and thus literary authority.

Therefore, and particularly given that Egerton herself eschews any explicit identification of the narrator's gender, the most productive position must surely be to follow her lead and eschew any attempt definitively to identify the narrator as either male or female, since the ambiguity around the gender of the narrator is a crucial part of what I will argue makes this story such a telling intervention into discourses of authority and writerliness, particularly where they intersect with gender, at this point in British literary and cultural history. Having said this, I will refer to the narrator as male in the course of this essay. This is primarily for polemical effect: referring to the narrator as male throws into relief my argument that there is a gendered tension at the heart of this story which relies on a normative depiction of the literary genius as masculine–and thus, most likely in this context, male. But I would invite readers to see the terms "male", "he", and so on, here, as if in scare quotes. Egerton's refusal explicitly to articulate her narrator's gender position is a key element in what I argue is her thoroughgoing problematization of the concept of masculine literary authority in this story.

My reading of the narrator as masculinized is linked to a second crucial aspect of Egerton's narrative. There is, throughout, an ironic distance set up between the dramatized, first-person narrator and the implied author, as I will go on to indicate (for example, the narrator uses absurdly overblown and bombastic language to describe his own anticipated achievements; he also expresses disgust for a figure who closely resembles Egerton herself, clearly implying that Egerton is not identifying herself with her narrator).[4] Thus, while the piece can fairly be described, *per* Hamerton, as about "a literary disappointment", it is not at all obvious with what seriousness readers are supposed to take this disappointment. We assume that the author of the story would, as a writer, be genuinely put out by a literary disappointment. Yet the way that the narrator is gently mocked throughout the story seems to invite the reader to concur with Hamerton that it is "*merely* a literary disappointment" (my emphasis), of no great import. This distance between narrator and implied author bolsters my argument that the narrator is being set up as in some way the author's "other", not least in terms of gender. However, the self-reflexive gesture of having a writer as the central character brings author and narrator into proximity, thus generating a tension within this relationship–is the attitude of author to narrator antagonistic, or empathetic? Like the ambiguity over the gender of the narrator, this tension is ultimately irresolvable, and itself implies an anxiety about the status of literary writing. Buried in this ambivalent relationship between implied author and narrator we might detect Egerton grappling with the question of what claims literary writing might be able to make for its wider social and cultural impact, a point I will return to in my conclusion.

I am, evidently, going to disagree with Hamerton's overall assessment of "A Lost Masterpiece". On the contrary, I will argue that this story of "a literary disappointment" turns out to be extremely fruitful. Firstly, I examine the way in which literary inspiration is itself described in the story, and compare this with the reflections of one of Egerton's contemporaries, Robert Louis Stevenson, on this process or experience. I then go on to indicate how this experience or process, part of what defines a writer as such, is inflected through gender in the text by examining closely the relationship between the narrator and the women he encounters, paying particular attention to the key female figure who, in Hamerton's words, "chases away" the narrator's "bright idea". This discussion will come to rest on what is also a jumping-off point, where I posit the importance to *fin-de-siècle* or early modernist literature of a particular conceptual nexus: that is, the relationship between work, women (or gender), and writing.[5]

Inspiration as Process and Egerton's Elf

Firstly, we should investigate what constitutes what I am calling the narrator's "inspiration" (since Egerton herself never actually uses the term). Four key images or metaphors appear as part of the narrator's description of this experience: the web, the pearl, the child, and the "elf". The first three images, the web, the pearl and the child, have more in common with each other than it might at first appear. Let us begin with the "fanciful web" being "spun" out of "delicate inner threads" (190), which is distinguished from the "outer self" that takes in, without (supposedly) analyzing, the details of the outside world. What is striking here is the use of a characteristically feminine activity to describe this process. Penelope's weaving is an obvious connotation, especially when the narrator goes on to congratulate himself on how he will "reveal to [the passers-by] the golden threads in the sober city woof" (193). We also cannot help but be reminded of Freud's "Femininity", where he muses on a possible relationship between women's only technical innovations, plaiting and weaving, and their desire to "weave" pubic hair to hide the shame of their genital lack (132). The use by a masculine narrator of this exemplarily–indeed, *per* Freud, definitively–feminine activity, to describe his own psychic activity, this narrator having been created by a female author, who herself used a male pseudonym, generates layers–or, better, a web–of gender disruption that is crucial in destabilizing narrative authority in this text.

The web mutates a few pages on into a "pearl", a "precious little pearl of a thought [...] evolving slowly out of the inner chaos" (193). A pearl is beautiful, certainly, and natural; but at its heart is a piece of grit (or, according to modern science, a parasite). Thus it is a paradoxical object; it is perfect, but can only arise where there has been contamination. Literary inspiration relies, perhaps, on some kind of irritation or disruption. When the narrator goes on to describe his pearl as "a priceless possession, not to be bartered for the Jagersfontein diamond" (193), a further characteristic springs to mind: a pearl reaches perfection in its natural state, unlike a diamond that must be cut and is thus to some extent man-made. The pearl goes on to reproduce spontaneously, to become "a whole quarrelet of pearls"–"Oriental pearls", of course (194). This pearl not only has the capacity to multiply itself, but we are also here reminded that it is unclear when a pearl may be said to be finished. A tiny pearl may be as perfect in its way as a large one; left to grow, does it become more perfect? Thus the pearl and the web taken together emphasize that what is being described is a process, not a moment. The idea emphatically does not come to the narrator all at once, in an ecstatic moment of inspiration. Rather it takes time to form; it is "spun into a fanciful web" (190), recorded in "delicate sure brushwork" (191); even by the time the "murderer" of the idea is first seen, the idea is still "evolving" (193), not complete and whole.

To round off this triumvirate of metaphors, we have the familiar comparison of a new idea with a new life, encapsulated in the ready-made phrase "brain-child". The narrator calls his idea "this darling brain-child, this offspring of my fancy, this rare little creation, perhaps embryo of genius that was my very own", and then "this dainty elusive birthling of my brain" (193). This further emphasizes that in this discourse of inspiration an idea must develop, evolve, rather than simply arriving fully formed all at once, since like a child it must pass through this "embryo" stage, be nurtured and given time to develop. And again, childbirth is, of course, inextricably associated with women. However, in keeping with the gender ambivalence of the narrator, the phrase "birthling of my brain" also evokes the image of Athene springing fully formed from the forehead of Zeus.[6] The female capacity for reproduction is, in this myth, arrogated by the male; such myths function to shore up male authority in the face of the power of female generativity. Egerton's choice of figurative language here draws attention to the gender anxiety implicit in key metaphors of literary inspiration.[7]

It is here that the story comes closest to the vocabulary and themes most familiar to readers of Egerton's other work. In stories such as "A Cross Line" and "The Spell of the White Elf" Egerton is much concerned with the physiological and psychological effects of pregnancy and childbirth on women. Egerton's explorations of female sexuality and physicality were radical for her time, and childbirth and motherhood emerge as integral to her understanding of femininity. Nicole Fluhr has drawn attention to the way in which Egerton depicts motherhood specifically in relation to writing, arguing that she "advocates a synthesis in which mothers' passionate engagement tempers and is tempered by artists' aesthetic and analytical detachment" (245). My reading of "A Lost

Masterpiece" might, however, appear to run counter to Fluhr's argument that Egerton's work "imagin[es] a mode of reproduction in which men play the most marginal of roles" (245), since I argue that in this story we see a masculine narrator experiencing something akin to childbirth in the process of literary inspiration. By contrast, actual mothers are evoked in negative terms by way of juxtaposition: on the last in a line of "grimy" barges that pass by the steamer on which he is travelling, Egerton's narrator tells us that "a woman sits suckling her baby, and a terrier with badly cropped ears yaps at us as we pass...." (191). The nursing mother is thus associated with dirt, mutilation and the bodily. What remains, however, is a connection between the process involved in, albeit anterior to, writing–that is, inspiration–and an experience which approximates childbirth. By allowing a masculine writer to have this experience, Egerton is, at the very least, positing a refiguring of the idea of maternity in terms of its relationship to literary creation, which is at a broad level precisely that to which Fluhr is drawing our attention. While this story does not, unlike so many of Egerton's stories, focus on the maternal, reproductive female body, it remains, thus, emphatically a presence as a key metaphor for, perhaps even the *sine qua non*, of creativity.

There are two key points, then, to make at this stage about the range of images used to describe what happens when an idea for a literary work arises. Firstly, the emphasis is squarely on process, and this, it seems to me, is exactly what Egerton is trying to express about an experience of literary inspiration. That we never know exactly what the narrator's idea is amplifies this sense that process, rather than content, is key. Secondly, the images I have discussed are all associated with femininity, and yet are, I argue, presented through a masculine narrator. Thus the gendering of literary inspiration is challenged. While masculine literary and cultural authority relies on an association between inspiration and masculinity, the metaphors used by Egerton in this story to describe her narrator's experience undermine these associations, and, by implication, the authority which they seek to insure.

There is, however, yet another narrative layer to consider. The images of the web, pearl and child are further mediated in the person of what the narrator calls "The elf that lurks in some inner cell" (191). It is this elf, it seems, who is in fact doing the weaving, placing the brushstrokes, producing the running comment that generates the "pearl" of the idea. Elves and the like appear regularly in Egerton's fiction, most frequently to describe either a child or a fragile-looking young woman. For example, in "The Spell of the White Elf", the "white elf" of the title is a baby girl who is taken in and treated as her own by an independent working woman writer. What the story emphasizes, however, is the woman's lack of conventional maternal feelings–she loves the child, is fascinated by it and kind to it, but throughout sees it as something mysterious, even magical, rather than something naturally hers or taken-for-granted–hence it is referred to throughout, and apparently quite seriously, as an "elf". Thus, while the whimsy associated with the word might make it difficult for contemporary readers, we see that, for Egerton, it seems usefully to convey something which is mysterious and inexplicable.

Comparison with another *fin de siècle* author, with whom Egerton might seem to have little in common, will be of assistance in focusing on the specific use Egerton makes of the "inner elf" here. Robert Louis Stevenson uses an image strikingly similar to Egerton's "inner elf" in an essay of 1892 entitled "A Chapter on Dreams". In this essay, which basically purports to describe Stevenson's own experience of literary (or indeed not-so-literary) inspiration, Stevenson posits the existence of "little people", or "some Brownie, some familiar", who, sometimes in collaboration with the author, and sometimes totally independently, come up with the idea for a story, often presenting it in the form of a dream (187). The writer–in this case, Stevenson himself–will awake from a dream to find that the building-blocks of a plot have been generated by these "little people" (sometimes plural, sometimes singular). The writer will then usually amend the story slightly to make it suitable for public consumption. This is particularly because, Stevenson says, "my Brownies have not a rudiment of what we call a conscience" (188); so, for example Stevenson had to add the "moral" elements of *The Strange Case of Dr. Jekyll and Mr. Hyde* himself (though he does not detail what these were). Stevenson's "little people" may begin as part of an extended metaphor, first appearing as "the little people who manage man's internal theatre" (182), but by the end of the essay Stevenson has developed his Brownies into beings which themselves have fully developed personalities–or rather, a collective personality; they are, he says "somewhat fantastic, like their stories hot and hot, full of passion and the picturesque, alive with animating incident; and they have no prejudice against the supernatural" (189). Similarly, Egerton's "elf", while less fully developed than Stevenson's, appears as multi-talented and vividly alive, as we see in this litany of active verbs in the continuous present describing its activity: "now throwing [...] now recording [...] touching [...] making" (Egerton, "A Lost Masterpiece", 191). In both instances, the labor of inspiration is carried out by highly active and industrious semi-mythical beings, which are both internal to the writer himself and markedly separate from him.

What, then, is at stake in making this claim, that one's literary inspiration is, in some senses, not one's own, though it comes from inside oneself? Firstly, it is worth noting that this model brings us back to the reproductive female body. Glossing Kristeva's discussion of pregnancy, Fluhr notes that for mothers-to-be, "their future children are both them and not-them"; (248) in a very concrete sense, not their own, but coming from inside them. This reinforces the absent presence of the maternal body here as central to Egerton's conception of inspiration. But there are a number of further ways in which this paradoxical figure might be read. Stephen Arata draws attention to the obvious Freudian reading of Stevenson's essay–the description of the Brownies as "hot and hot, full of passion", and so forth, cries out to be read as the irruption of the id, of otherwise suppressed desires, through the respectable surface of the writer's personality. As Arata puts it, "It seems especially appropriate that Edward Hyde should spring from a dream, since like the Brownies he is so easily identified with the raging energies of the id" (48).[8] But, as Arata points out, the Brownies are also un-Freudian in that they have "developed what can only be called a business sense" (48); they have an eye to the dreamer-writer's bank-book, they respond to his economic need. Thus the responsibility for the dirty business of business, as well as of passion, the supernatural, the amoral, and so on, is more or less abdicated–that is the Brownie's realm, outside the control of the dreamer-writer. Most importantly for my purposes, both Egerton's and Stevenson's little people are emphatically connected with industriousness, with labor, with work: Egerton introduces her "elf" by saying that it (the gender is unclear) is "very busy" (191); Stevenson's little people "labour all night long" (183). My assumption is, therefore, that there is something important about the writer (by this I mean Egerton's narrator, Stevenson's dreamer) distancing himself from work, from labor. The obvious model is that of the distinction between the capitalist and the worker. While the former may have authority, the latter, ultimately, has power–to down tools if nothing else. Thus it is in the mind of the writer; it is as if the writer-capitalist has to placate his brownie-elf-workers by acknowledging and containing their power, and thus retaining his authority.

This figuring of literary inspiration as requiring a distance from, and indeed regulatory censoring of, the (potentially chaotic) contributions of the "workers" indicates a more general anxiety in British literary culture of the time about the perceived threats posed to literary authority by the increasing professionalization of writing.[9] No-one expressed this anxiety more vividly than Stevenson himself. One might have expected him to welcome wholeheartedly the success of *Dr. Jekyll and Mr. Hyde*, which gave him financial independence and liberated him from his father's oppressive control. However, Stevenson was so distressed at the idea of writing professionally that, in a letter to Edmund Gosse, Stevenson says that "we [professional authors] are whores, some of us are pretty, some are not", and "like prostitutes [we] live by a pleasure" (cited in Arata, 49). The prostitute is, of course, the Ur-working women. Stevenson's analogies thus bring together the class dimension of this anxiety with its gender dimension, and map onto a tension which has been observed in the literary culture of the period; that is, as Elana Gomel has put it with reference to Oscar Wilde, in "the challenge to the (male) *auteur* presented by the (female) popular hack" (78). The image of the "(female) popular hack" was of course itself a product of the professionalization of writing during this period, and the concomitant increase in female writers. Female hacks appear in stories such as Henry James's "The Next Time", also published in *The Yellow Book*, in order to be distinguished from the struggling male literary genius. While the literary genius, in James's story, ultimately fails, we are clearly encouraged to sympathize with him and sneer at the successful female author of three-decker novels, which sit on her shelves like–of course–"sets of triplets" (227). There are no characters explicitly identified as female hacks in Egerton's story; but there are a number of women who, at various levels, present a challenge to the masculine literary authority embodied in the narrator. Those who present the strongest challenge are, as I will go on to discuss, in some ways analogous to the female hack (and indeed the prostitute) in being, explicitly or implicitly, working women, and in one case a working woman with a particularly difficult (difficult for the narrator, that is) relationship with writing.

The Women of "A Lost Masterpiece"

The first women in Egerton's story appear alongside the narrator on the river steamer, and are characterized by elements stereotypically (and indeed misogynistically) associated with women. The first is revealed gradually, as if in the corner of the narrator's eye, through the "hideous green" of her "velveteen [...] sleeves" (Egerton, "A Lost Masterpiece", 190), the language mocking women's vain and superficial interest in clothing, yet at the same time asserting the narrator's expertise (he can identify the material as velveteen) and judgment (the green is "hideous") in this area. The "young ladies" on the narrator's other side are equally scathingly represented, the three key phrases being "supercilious giggle", "audible remarks" and "personal appearance" (190). Again, women's superficiality is emphasized, as well as, here, their inappropriate behavior–

one could imagine the phrases appearing in an etiquette manual for young ladies, describing behavior to be avoided (and doubtless associated with the lower classes). Thus Egerton deftly outlines her narrator's negative view of women. But while he judges them and looks down at them, at the same time he is himself aware of being looked at, remarked upon, and judged; on the surface, the narrator asserts his authority, but ultimately he cannot control the extent to which he is himself an object of scrutiny.

Having descended from the boat, the narrator then smiles at "a pretty anaemic city girl" (192). However, this smile turns immediately to antagonism; the narrator "only remembered that she was a stranger when she flashed back an indignant look of affected affront" (192). We note that the affront is only "affected"–like the girls on the steamer, this woman is superficial; the narrator sees through her attempt to perform the socially suitable response, and if the affront is only "affected" then her genuine response is, the narrator implies, doubtless one of gratification on having been smiled at by this man-about-town. The last word is given on this encounter when the narrator makes, significantly, his only explicit utterance in the whole story: he dismisses this moment of social awkwardness, and with it the woman herself, by saying "'Go thy way, little city maid, get thee to thy typing.'" (193). If it comes to affectation, this is rather a case of the pot calling the kettle black, as the use of the archaic "thou" form, together with the pastoral formulation "little [...] maid", only serves to reinforce the image of a rather self-satisfied dandy, bound up with his sense of creative genius, and finally calling out to an unknown woman in the street in cod-Spenserian terms. The picture is frankly absurd, even in the context of Egerton's tendency to melodrama in some of her dialogue, and reinforces the distinction between the narrator and the implied author. The use of "thou" also, of course, implies intimacy, which reinforces my reading of this as an exchange between (masculine) sexual predator and (feminine) prey–albeit where the potential victim is ready to show her claws.

Most interesting for my purposes, the "city maid" is dismissed to her "typing." This tells us a great deal about how the narrator perceives this woman. She is, firstly, utterly modern and, symbolically at least, in the vanguard of gender politics. As Leah Price and Pamela Thurschwell have recently put it in their collection of essays on secretaries, "turn-of-the-century feminists associated standing up for one's rights with sitting down at one's desk" (4). She is also thus independent, probably unmarried, and needs to work for a living. She is therefore the kind of woman at whom it is legitimate to shout in the street: "As a typist," Morag Shiach notes, "the woman worker becomes available, visible and sexualised" (77). Finally, if she is a typist, she presents a profound challenge to the category of "writer". Price and Thurschwell make the point that the advent of the typewriter reinforced the separation of the mechanical, physical process of writing from the cognitive process required in its composition. Indeed, they note, "[i]t could be objected that nothing but semantic coincidence links 'writing' in the sense of producing material marks with 'writing' in the sense of composing verbal content" (2). Certainly the figure of the dictation secretary drives a wedge between these two senses of the term. Price and Thurschwell encapsulate this distinction where they cite Truman Capote's dismissive remark on Jack Kerouac, "That's not writing. That's typing", and gloss it thus: "The opposite of genius is typist" (2). And yet, typing does remain fundamentally a form of writing; this might be only in the sense of "producing material marks", writing of the mechanical variety, but, of course, it cannot be restricted to this kind of writing, and may also include "composing verbal content".

Returning to our narrator, we find that we can shed light on this overdetermined articulation of his superiority–"Go thy way little city maid, get thee to thy typing"–by viewing it as a response to the threatening presence of another writer; for, as I have indicated, the typist must be a writer of a sort. In order to insure his genius, the narrator must distinguish himself from this "little city maid": by using the familiar, and indeed literary, "thou" form; by sending her on *her* way, to be distinguished from his; and most importantly, by identifying her as a "typist"–genius's other. There is also some anxiety aroused, perhaps, by her "affected" affront. Typists, ideally, do not pay attention to content, but mechanically transcribe whatever is being dictated, or set out before them in longhand. But this one is, apparently, a dissembler; what does this imply for her relationship to her employers' texts? Does she "affect" not to read what she is writing, when all the while she is in fact reading it and, perhaps, contaminating it? The women the narrator comes across are thus becoming increasingly challenging; the ill-dressed lady and the giggling girls were easily dismissed, it seems, but this "little" typist has generated the need for a rather more emphatic assertion of difference.

The next woman our *flâneur* encounters will be even harder to see off. Having mounted a bus, a "foreign element" (Egerton, "A Lost Masterpiece", 194) passes across the narrator's field of vision, in the form of a hurrying woman. This woman infuriates the narrator by hurrying along the pavement and never being finally overtaken by the bus on which he is sitting. He seems unable to ignore her presence, and indeed the sight of her "recalls" something to him, an exotic scene at the Corcovado (195). Yet he is unable to work out why this woman should evoke this image, and it is this inability to work out the connection that seems ultimately to be fatal to his literary idea. In particular, he becomes fixated on the word "*pompier*", from a song in French that is being sung in the exotic landscape evoked by the sight of this woman (195). He is himself in the dark about the meaning of the word, asking "What in the world is a *pompier*?" (195), but is "convinced *pompier* expresses her in some subtle way–absurd word!" (196). As Ana Parejo Vadillo has explained in her discussion of "A Lost Masterpiece", "'L'art pompier,' or official art, is a term applied to the nineteenth-century French neoclassic tendencies in painting. By extension, the term refers to any literary work that is outmoded, pretentious or ridiculous" (24). Parejo Vadillo goes on to argue that the narrator thus "seems to suggest that the figure of the *flâneuse*/streetwalker is outmoded" (24), by comparison with the narrator's own highly modern use of river steamer and omnibus. However, this reading does not take account of the ironic distance between narrator and author in this story, alluded to in my introduction, which I can now flesh out.

As I noted above, the narrator's response to the hurrying woman does not comply with the standard *flâneur/passante* relationship in that she murders his thought rather than providing inspiration. In a further modification of the standard model, here the narrator's fascination with the woman is characterized by disgust; far from being entranced by her beauty, he is repelled by the woman's "elbowing gait, and tight skirt shortened to show her great splay feet" (196), drawing attention to her physicality (and in so doing perhaps evincing a misogynistic disgust at the female body already indicated in the narrator's description of the breast-feeding mother, mentioned above). In particular, it is the woman's pace that distresses the narrator: "It annoyed me, for I could not help wondering why she was in such a desperate hurry" (194). The woman is described as ugly, busy, intrusive, even somewhat masculine. She thus fully complies with contemporary negative stereotypes of the New Woman; indeed, *Punch*'s cartoon of a New Woman sitting legs akimbo on a throne, brandishing the key to learning and reading Ibsen, was apparently based on Egerton herself, and was produced in the issue of 28 April 1894 precisely as a response to the publication of *The Yellow Book* (De Vere White, 28). It is here that the ironic distance between implied author and narrator is particularly evident: Egerton is unlikely, we assume, to be identifying wholeheartedly with a narrator who is repulsed by a character which resembles her, or a category of persons she is supposed to exemplify. If, then, we place the use of the term *pompier* in this context, we might note that Egerton has in fact been building up a picture of the narrator himself to which the term would be entirely apt. The level of his pretension has, for example, been expressed a few paragraphs before where he rails against the woman's disruption of his "web of genius, undoubted genius" (Egerton, "A Lost Masterpiece", 194), that "is to bring *me* kudos and make countless thousands rejoice" (195). The analysis is, perhaps, simple: we see in others what we most fear in ourselves. By insisting that the word *"pompier"* is associated with this ugly, hurrying woman, the narrator is distancing himself from the possibility that his genius, his "work", is bombastic, pretentious, and thus valueless.[10]

Parejo Vadillo goes on helpfully to articulate the paradox at the heart of this story; namely, that while railing against the woman's having "murdered" his story, "the omnibus rider 'finds' a new masterpiece (i.e. the story we are reading), which, strangely enough, restores to the *flâneuse*/streetwalker her heroic character" (24). While acknowledging the validity of this argument, and agreeing that some affirmation of the walking woman is thus implied, I suggest that there are two problems with Parejo Vadillo's reading. Firstly, this apparent inscription of the walking woman as hero(ine) of the story cannot neutralize the negative gender stereotypes to which Egerton draws our attention throughout the story. Secondly, and most importantly, her description of the New Woman walker as *flâneuse* obscures the distinction between this hurrying female character and the narrator.

Certainly, recent scholarship has challenged the idea that *flânerie* is an exclusively male category. Deborah L. Parsons's *Streetwalking the Metropolis* is the most important critical work in this regard; Parsons insists that the concept of the *flâneuse* is not, as previous scholars such as Janet Wolff had insisted, "rendered impossible by the sexual divisions of the nineteenth century" (cited in Parsons, 4). This does not, however, mean that the *flâneur* and the *flâneuse* perform exactly the same activity, being different in gender only. (Indeed, Parejo Vadillo's qualification *"flâneuse*/streetwalker" indicates her own caution around the use of the term.) On the contrary, as Parsons notes, "a mode of expression can be seen to develop in the late nineteenth and early twentieth centuries that emphasizes observation of the city yet is distinct from the characteristic practice of the authoritative *flâneur*, comparable instead to the marginalized urban familiarity of the rag-picker" (6). However, while positing the possibility of an alternative *flânerie*, Parsons agrees that both *flâneur* and *flâneuse* are characterized by their "observation of the city". This is certainly what the narrator is engaged in; however, he figures the walking woman as doing the opposite–hurrying along "untiringly", oblivious to her surroundings.

Further, Parsons observes that there remains an identifiable set of practices which defined, at this point, the "authoritative *flâneur*" (6). Among the most important of these are the *flâneur*'s sauntering pace and his purposelessness. This is made clear in, for example, Rachel Bowlby's classic discussion of the *flâneur*, and in particular her analysis of Louis Huart's 1850 text *Le flâneur* in which Huart explicitly excludes from the category of *flâneur* he "who walks fast" (198). Parsons too notes that "The *flâneur* walks idly through the city, listening to its narrative" (3). Indiscriminate wandering, idling, listening to the narrative of the city–its "life-throbs" (Egerton, "A Lost Masterpiece", 196)–are certainly behaviors displayed by the narrator. By contrast, the hurrying woman would seem to have some purpose, some clear aim in mind, something to achieve, perhaps. Indeed, it is the woman's pace one which first caught the narrator's attention by arousing his annoyance: "It annoyed me," he says, "for I could not help wondering why she was in such a desperate hurry" (194). He goes on to ask himself "What is she hurrying for? We can't escape her" (196), and finally laments that "My brain is void, all is dark within; the flowers are faded, the music stilled; the lovely illusive little being has flown, and yet she pounds along untiringly" (196), revealing the extent of his egocentricity as he marvels that she keeps walking even after she has achieved this murder–this must have been her aim, he implies, so what can her purpose in continuing to hurry possibly be? Therefore, even taking into account Parson's critique of the idea of an exclusively male *flânerie*, Egerton's hurrying woman remains, in terms of her function within the story, the diametric opposite of the traditional *flâneur*.

The distinction between the insouciant, wandering male writer, strolling around the city in the confident hope of receiving inspiration from his "elf", and the woman striding purposefully along in pursuit of some specific end, maps directly onto the tension between "the (male) *auteur*" or genius and "(female) popular hack" discussed above. Thus, while the hurrying, purposeful woman of Egerton's story is not necessarily a writer, she is certainly contiguous with a discourse which, in the era of art for art's sake, seems to have constructed women's (paid) work as purposeful, and thus not only contaminated, but potentially contaminating. As we have seen, it is elves, or Brownies, who conduct the morally dubious, difficult, laborious "work" which forms the foundation for, while being emphatically distinct from, the morally refined, authoritative "work" of the writer proper. Further, we remember that the metaphors Egerton employs in her story to express the elf's work are dense with associations of femininity, revealing the (female, proletarian) power on which the writer's authority relies. Set in this context, it is hardly surprising to find that in Egerton's story, typists, hurrying women–women with jobs, with a purpose, who work–are potentially fatally threatening to masculine genius.

***

As Egerton's story draws to a close, it continues gently to mock its narrator, but also seems to involve some self-mockery on Egerton's part:

> Does she realise what she has done? She has trampled a rare little mind-being unto death, destroyed a precious literary gem. Aye, one that, for aught I know, might have worked a revolution in modern thought; added a new human document to the archives of man; been the keystone to psychic investigations; solved problems that lurk in the depths of our natures and tantalise us with elusive gleams of truth; heralded in, perchance, the new era; when such simple problems as Home Rule, Bimetallism, or the Woman Question will be mere themes for school-board compositions—who can tell? (196)

The absurdly overblown ambition of the narrator is revealed as he builds clause after clause, imagining giddier and yet giddier heights of achievement for the lost literary gem. And yet, the underlying question seems to be one which, surely, must concern all writers–must have concerned Egerton herself–namely, what is the work that literature can do? The literary piece might, the narrator supposes, have "worked a revolution"–answered the Woman Question, no less. But the paragraph raises the question of what kind of "work" writing is, ultimately–compared to, for example, the work of the typist, or indeed the prostitute. As a working woman writer, Egerton certainly distances herself from her pompous narrator. And yet she must, to some extent, also be identifying with him as a fellow literary writer (or someone who aspires to be one)– implying that she in turn distances herself from, for example, the "little city" typist, or even the figure of the bustling New Woman. We thus return to my suggestion that, whatever the gender of the a writer, they must perform a particular kind of masculinity, one that clearly distinguishes them from working women, in order to be able to figure themselves as experiencing the inspiration that insures a work of literature. But Egerton's refusal in her story explicitly to articulate the gender position of her narrator, together with this varying degree of ironic distance between narrator and implied author, finally undermines any attempt firmly to locate narrative "authority" within this highly experimental text. In so doing, "A Lost Masterpiece" reveals and challenges the gendered, class-based limitations of "socially sanctioned images of authorship" (Clark 33) in the literature and culture of the period.

Works cited

Arata, Stephen. *Fictions of Loss in the Victorian* fin-de-siècle. Cambridge: Cambridge University Press, 1996.

Booth, Wayne. "Distance and Point of View: An essay in classification." *Essentials of the Theory of Fiction.* Ed. Michael J. Hoffman and Patrick D. Murphy. London: Leicester University Press, 1996. 116-133.

Bowlby, Rachel. *Feminist Destinations and Further Essays on Virginia Woolf.* Edinburgh: Edinburgh University Press, 1997.

de Vere White, Terence. *A Leaf from the Yellow Book: The Correspondence of George Egerton.* London: The Richards Press, 1958.

Egerton, George. "A Cross Line." *Keynotes and Discords.* Ed. Sally Ledger. London: Continuum, 2006. 3-14.

—. "A Lost Masterpiece: A City Mood, Aug. '93." *The Yellow Book* 1 (April 1894): 189-196.

—. "The Spell of the White Elf." *Keynotes and Discords.* Ed. Sally Ledger. London: Continuum, 2006. 25-31.

Fluhr, Nicole. "Figuring the New Woman: Writers and Mothers in George Egerton's Early Stories." *Texas Studies in Literature and Language* 43.3 (2001): 243-266.

Freud, Sigmund. "Femininity." *New Introductory Lectures on Psychoanalysis and Other Works.* Vol. 22. London: Hogarth, 1932-36. 112-135.

Gilbert, Sandra M., and Susan Gubar. *The Madwoman in the Attic: The Woman Writer and the Nineteenth-Century Literary Imagination.* New Haven: Yale University Press, 1979.

Gomel, Elana. "Oscar Wilde, *The Picture of Dorian Gray*, and the (Un)Death of the Author." *Narrative* 12 (2004): 74-92.

Hamerton, Philip Gilbert. "The Yellow Book Criticised." *The Yellow Book* 2 (July 1894).

James, Henry. "The Next Time." *Collected Stories.* Vol. 2. London: Everyman, 1999. 223-263.

Leger, Sally. *The New Woman: Fiction and feminism at the fin de siècle.* Manchester: Manchester University Press, 1997.

McCullough, Kate. "Mapping the '*Terra Incognita*' of Woman: George Egerton's *Keynotes* (1893) and New Woman Fiction." *The New Nineteenth Century: Feminist Readings of Underread Victorian Fiction.* Ed. Barbara Leah Harman and Susan Meyer. New York: Garland, 1996. 205-223.

Parejo Vadillo, Ana. *Women Poets and Urban Aestheticism: Passengers of Modernity*. Basingstoke: Palgrave Macmillan, 2005.

Parsons, Deborah L. *Streetwalking the Metropolis: Women, the City and Modernity*. Oxford: Oxford University Press, 2000.

Price, Leah and Pamela Thurschwell. *Literary Secretaries/Secretarial Culture*. Aldershot: Ashgate, 2005.

Shiach, Morag. *Modernism, Labour and Selfhood in British Literature and Culture, 1890 – 1930*. Cambridge: Cambridge University Press, 2004.

Stetz, Margaret. "*New Grub Street* and the Woman Writer of the 1890s." *Transforming Genres: New Approaches to British Fiction of the 1890s*. Ed. Nikki Lee Manos and Meri-Jane Rochelson. New York: St Martin's Press, 1994. 21-45.

Stetz, Margaret, and Mark Samuels Lasner. *The Yellow Book: A Centenary Exhibition*. Cambridge: The Houghton Library, 1994.

Stevenson, Robert Louis. "A Chapter on Dreams." *The Works of Robert Louis Stevenson*. Vol. 16. London: Chatto & Windus, 1912. 177-189.

Turner, Mark W. "Urban Encounters and Visual Play in the *Yellow Book*." *Encounters in the Victorian Press: Editors, Authors, Readers*. Ed. Laurel Brake and Julie F. Codell. Basingstoke: Palgrave Macmillan, 2005.

Woolf, Virginia. *A Room of One's Own*. London: Penguin, 1945.

Zakreski, Patricia. *Representing Female Artistic Labour, 1848-1890: Refining Work for the Middle-Class Woman*. Aldershot: Ashgate, 2006.

Notes

[1] My attendance at the conference where I presented the paper that formed the material for this chapter was funded by an Overseas Conference Grant from the British Academy, whose generous support I would like to acknowledge here. I am also grateful for the helpful comments on earlier drafts of this article from Kate Macdonald and Kate Briggs, and for the feedback from those who heard an earlier version of this paper at the English, Communication, Film and Media seminar series, Anglia Ruskin University, 15 November 2006.

[2] Any use of the term *flâneur* with reference to gender needs to take account of Deborah Parsons's argument that "the concept of the *flâneur* itself contains gender ambiguities that suggest the figure to be a site for the contestation of male authority rather than the epitome of it" (5-6). Nevertheless, Parsons agrees that the literature and culture of the time presents us with a "characteristic practice of the authoritative *flâneur*" (6). This authoritative *flâneur*, susceptible to contestation

though he may be, is figured primarily and normatively as male. As I will go on to argue, in this story Egerton mobilises just such a normative depiction of the *flâneur* precisely in order to expose its faultlines and challenge the assumptions on which it is based.

[3] For a description of this relationship, see Bowlby, chapter 13.

[4] I am using Wayne Booth's classic taxonomy of types of narrator (summarised in Booth).

[5] I say "*fin-de-siècle or* early modernist" because I am interested in the suggestion that Egerton can be seen as fitting either of these literary categories. For example, in her book on New Woman writers Sally Ledger has suggested that "Egerton's short stories have characteristics which we would now associate with a modernist literary aesthetic: they are compressed, elliptical, impressionistic rather than explanatory, and focus on the inner consciousness of their female subjects" (187) (although of course part of what is interesting about "A Lost Masterpiece" is that, unusually, it does not focus on the "inner consciousness of [...] a female [subject]". There is not space here for a fuller exploration of the ways in which her work forms part of, or indeed challenges, current literary historical categories, except to say that Egerton's radical subject matter as well as, most importantly, her experimental prose, bears striking continuities with key modernist figures such as, most obviously, Virginia Woolf. For example, Woolf's *A Room of One's Own* famously describes the same situation but with the gender positions reversed, where a female narrator has her idea driven "into hiding" by the gesticulations of a Beadle, embodiment of masculine authority (8). Another key aspect of Woolf's text, of course, the playful slipperiness of her narrative voice – "(call me Mary Beton, Mary Seton, Mary Carmichael or by any name you please [...])" (7); thus while Woolf's text presents a more overt engagement with feminist issues than this one of Egerton's (though other of Egerton's texts are, of course, explicitly feminist in content) they share the use of an ambiguously defined narrator to generate a text which, in both instances, challenges simply binary definitions of gender.

[6] I am grateful to Kate Macdonald for drawing my attention to this resonance.

[7] See Zakreski 118-28 for a discussion of the relationship between the discourse of motherhood and the figuring of, specifically, the woman writer in the mid to late Victorian period.

[8] Sandra M. Gilbert and Susan Gubar have made this Freudian connection, but linked it specifically to gender, when noting the prevalence of what must be close relations of the Brownie or elf among women writers of the nineteenth century: "the desirous little creatures so many woman writers have recorded encountering in the haunted glens of their own minds, hurrying scurrying furry ratlike *its* or *ids*, inescapable *incubi*" (570).

[9] The founding of the Society of Authors by Walter Besant in 1884 is perhaps the most obvious indicator of this trend toward professionalization.

[10] Modern readers might of course initially translate the phrase as "I am the real fireman / the only fireman". While this is an unlikely primary meaning in this context, perhaps it is possible to find a playful connection between the hurrying

woman and the word "fireman". She is, as I note elsewhere, described in somewhat masculine terms; and perhaps her hurrying evokes the phrase "where's the fire"?

Chapter Two

Pursuing Political Power by Being Physically Powerful: The Autobiography of Lillian M. Faithfull, New Woman

Tracy Collins

In 1925 Lillian Faithfull published her autobiography *In the House of My Pilgrimage*. Ms. Faithfull, Oxford graduate, lecturer in English literature at Holloway College, vice-principal at King's College, principal of Cheltenham Ladies' College, and long-time President of the All England Women's Hockey Association, was an advocate for improvement of education for girls in the British *fin de siècle*. She worked as a secretary in the war office, was an educator, an academic, and a world-class field hockey player. This particular author and this particular autobiography are not unique. Faithfull is a representative of the well-known extraordinary political and cultural personality that existed at the end of the nineteenth century--the New Woman. Faithfull is only one example of a politically progressive woman who describes in her autobiography an early interest in physical fitness, athletics, and sports while later demonstrating an independence of mind and lifestyle that defined the New Woman. She not only noticed the major role that games, athletics, and fitness had in her growing-up, but, in what amounted to a subversive intent, she also wrote her autobiography to advocate the same revolutionary social strategy for girls and women in general. In short, Faithfull used her autobiography not only as a testament but also as a guidebook to how women could resist patriarchal authority and gain political power by developing physical fitness and athleticism, a new empowerment of the female body. This body became the personality of her emancipated self.

Autobiography Theory and the Female Body

In light of the critical theory of women's life writing that has been produced until now, the question becomes, what can an extraction and framing of the sporting body described in autobiographies and memoirs by New Women add to that discussion? There are at least five answers to this question. First, analyzing such a text enriches the theoretical landscape by adding yet another layer of relevance to the neglected canon of women's autobiography, which it represents. Feminist scholarship on autobiography has been fertile, especially in the past fifteen years.[1] Yet no attempt has been made to inventory a collection of New Women autobiographies. Even so, studying the sporting athletic body described in autobiographies and memoirs by New Women is to question, perhaps confrontationally, the notion of a separate tradition of women's autobiographical writing established by earlier scholars. When such a collection is accomplished, it will confirm my conclusions in the analysis that follows that the New Woman is a special personality, and that special personality was an upper middle-class and upper-class woman who, in addition to possessing the advantage of an advanced cultural and political education, was essentially physically fit and engaged in athletics and sports.

A second reason for an analysis of the sporting athletic body described in autobiographies and memoirs by New Women is that it adds to the ongoing investigation of the construction of the female self. In dealing with any autobiography as a collection of historical fact, how a self is constructed is important, and the constructed self is a paramount matter of these New Woman texts. Primarily, the self that is being constructed is perceived as in quest of liberation, and their books prove that that self existed as a valid possibility in the time in which they were writing. As Susan Groag Bell and Marilyn Yalom note in their introduction to *Revealing Lives: Autobiography, Biography, and Gender* (1990), debates on autobiography have recently been based on post-structuralist theories that "deconstruct texts and decenter subjects so as to deny or at least question the familiar concept of a mimetic relationship between literature and life" (2). What is clear for women like Lillian Faithfull is that whether the life she is describing is real or not is not the question. It was imagined as a possibility in her lifetime, which is just as significant.[2] If the New Woman author of her life writing was the textual double of a real person, then the physically fit and athletic New Woman really existed. If the New Woman autobiographer is constructing a self, she is constructing a self that is active, athletic, and physically fit. More importantly for my study, the "self" that is reported, the active, athletic "self" that is revealed, would matter whether it was fictive or real. The confounding phenomenon of the sporting New Woman would be no less sensational.

A third reason to study the sporting athletic body described in autobiographies and memoirs by New Women is to question, again confrontationally, the "tradition" of women's autobiographical writing that early critics established. More recently Linda Peterson in her *Traditions of Victorian Women's Autobiography: The Poetics and Politics of Life Writing* (1999) considered this desire to create a female tradition. She agrees that "the argument about a separate (and singular) tradition of women's life writing is worth reexamining" (2).[3] Peterson answers this however, by claiming that she reconsiders "Victorian women's autobiography not by presupposing the existence of a women's tradition but instead by asking about possible self-representational modes available to, acknowledged, or created by women's writers" (3). Yet as her title *Traditions of Victorian Women's Autobiography* suggests, she is concerned with traditions. What Peterson does, however, is to propose traditions based not on gender but on "other allegiances religious, regional, political, or social" (2). My study of Faithfull and others discovers a category that might not have a place in Peterson's "allegiances." That is, a woman could have an "allegiance" to herself as an actualized body. It would not be, however, a body as a means for patriarchal reproduction agendas. It might not even be a body that represented physiologies that are patronized by males. My study of New Woman autobiographies, and Lillian Faithfull in particular, notices that one of the "allegiances" a woman could have while writing her autobiography was to her body. It recognizes how integral to a definition of self an interest in physical fitness and athletic activities is to these late Victorian women.

A fourth reason to study these texts has to do with the intentionality or goals of New Woman authors. In *Lives of Their Own* (1999), Martha Watson, in an attempt to examine the rhetoric of the autobiographies of famous women activists, notices that many women who wrote autobiographies did not need to write in order "to assert themselves as individuals" but instead were "were expressing the possibility of a new kind of womanhood for others" rather than themselves (2). The same is true for the large body of New Woman writers who authored the texts of this study in which Lillian Faithfull is an example. New Women, in writing their stories, were offering alternative narratives which other women could imagine for their lives. To my application of Watson's analysis must now be added crucial missing evidence. New Women were offering a personality whose essential newness specifically included a desire to be physically fit and athletic. To use Domna Stanton's phrase,

New Woman autobiographers created a "new female subject" (15). Beyond Stanton, the emphasis I would like to make about these new female subjects, however, is that the female subject had now become not only an actually real subject but also a physically active one. New Women wrote their life stories to record and recommend a lifestyle that was grounded in a new preference for health, active exercise and very often assertive athleticism.

What more can an analysis of the sporting athletic body described in autobiographies and memoirs by New Women offer? The final answer to this question must combine the description of the physical body of the New Woman and the current discourse of feminist body theory.[4] As Simone de Beauvoir, Judith Butler and more recently Sidonie Smith explain, "masculine disembodiment is only possible on the condition that women occupy their bodies as their essential and enslaving identities" and by defining women as *other*: "men are able through the shortcut of definition to dispose of their [women's] bodies, to make them other than their bodies and to make their bodies other than themselves" (*Subjectivity* 11).[5]

To effect a transgendered autobiographical discourse, theorists of female autobiography have worked on reclaiming the body from the ironic objectification of its traditional disembodiment and to relocate it in the position of the subject. Some have attacked the ways in which the female body has been overwritten by social constructions, while others focus on the multiplicity of bodies, thereby challenging the notion of any unified female body. Ultimately, theorists interested in autobiographies by women have begun to look for the ways in which the body emerges in, disrupts, or redirects narrative practices. For if economic and political realities are played out on the bodies of women, the signature of the political is erased when the reader does not attend to the body in the text. Simply put, the body must not be ignored. Properly put, the body must be privileged. It is, indeed, the entirety of the autobiographical object—certainly in any analysis that rejects dualist theories of human nature.

However, as Shirley Castelnuovo and Sharon Guthrie in *Feminism and the Female Body: Liberating the Amazon Within* (1998) find, feminist theorists who have set out to reclaim the female body do not escape a crippling emphasis on Cartesian dualism. The assumption underlying their theories "is that a focus on the body automatically results in a non-dualistic analysis. If we look closely at their liberatory analyses, however, we find that they have not actually done what they claim to do: eliminate dualism" (32). That is what happens for these theorists when they emphasize cognitive activities without realizing that in order to empower and encourage women cognitively they must be transformed physically: "Transformation of the female self requires bodily transformation as well. . . . The mind and body must be conceived of as a unity in understanding the social construction of gender and sexuality and in developing and embodying feminist perspectives" (32, 35).

With this goal in mind, Castelnuovo and Guthrie set out to "cultivate and celebrate an Amazonian presence among women" (1). They choose to rehabilitate and return respect to the "Amazon" personality. An Amazon they define as "a warrior," but not a warrior "with a blade or gun in hand." Instead they define her warrior-like qualities:

> As stemming from the fact that she has developed her bodily and mental skills to their fullest capacity and she directs her energies toward achieving equality for women. Consequently, she has the power and commitment to equalize the fields on which hierarchical gender relations are played out. Moreover, because she is aware of the need to protect herself physically, she has the potential to minimize, if not eliminate, the physical power imbalances between herself and the men with whom she interacts; and she knows that, when necessary, she has the right to defend herself. She is a woman who represents a significant challenge to patriarchal domination. (2)

They use the contemporary female body-builder as one example of this modern Amazon. They concur with analyses that find that women's competitive body-building is a singular site of female resistance to patriarchal constructions. The twenty-first century female body-builder/"Amazon," however, has an ancestor. The New Woman is characterized by physical fitness combined with mental fitness. These virtues were simultaneous in the New Woman or she was not a New Woman. The proposition of Castelnuovo and Guthrie has not been brought to the study of the New Woman. This makes existing studies to one degree or another fundamentally deficient. My examination of the case of Lillian Faithfull will illuminate the repercussions of this crucial oversight. By extension, it will suggest the need for an assembly of a more cogent theoretical foundation thus far absent in the assessment of the New Woman.

Reading the athletic and physically fit body in New Woman autobiographies is important because at a time in history when women's bodies were essentialized and bodies were literally asked by society to disappear into private invisibility, New Women chose to write life stories that not only brought attention to their physical bodies, but also explicitly named and assigned the ways that their bodies could be used and were being used as agents of emancipation and change. The body in these autobiographical texts was an instrument of subversive practice in pursuit of the political emancipation of the subject.

Lillian Faithfull's model of a physically active and healthy woman did not exist only in her autobiography. This model also existed with unintentionally attractive vitality in the pages of *Punch*. In it, women like Faithfull recognized and found a new costume to allow them a greater freedom of movement. Indeed, reading cartoons from *Punch* offered an inventory of the ways clothing and associated vestments changed to accommodate women's new engagement in sports so that the sporting costume of women became the uniquely signature costume of the New Woman. That *Punch* intended only to ridicule the New Woman by depicting her in sporting clothes did not matter. New Women ignored the ridicule and adopted the clothes. They were the vanguard of the movement of women that would reject slavery of all kids, including slavery to fashion.

A model of a physically fit, healthy, athletic, and intellectually assertive New Woman can be found in some of the representative writing—especially fiction--of the later Victorian age. Of the at least one hundred New Woman novels that can be clearly so identified, I have read almost thirty and they all offer late Victorian women a new athletic image of themselves. Scholars today can map many of the destabilizing effects these physically fit and athletic New Woman heroines had on their convention-bound readers. Therefore, to look at the truly pervasive sporting images and emphatically physical bodies of the heroines in New Woman fiction is to trace the cause and effect connection between a healthy, physically active fictive New Woman body and the upset of the traditional political paradigm against which real New Women struggled.[6]

Faithfull's Authoritative Body

An important goal of Faithfull's text is not only to offer a history of her exceptional life but also to advocate the need for revolutionary women's education at both the high school and university levels. Her autobiography however, begins with a gloss of the historical and cultural time into which she was born. She begins "Those of us who were born between 1860 and 1870 may indeed consider ourselves fortunate, for we have surely lived through the most interesting and eventful period for women in our national history" (3). After the larger cultural picture that she begins to paint with the first sentence, she moves specifically to women. "It has been a time of extraordinarily rapid change in the status of women, in their education, their social life, their work and their amusements" (3). These aspects of a woman's life that have so rapidly changed at the end of the nineteenth-century Faithfull will ultimately attribute to women being physically fit for the challenge.

The remainder of her introduction is spent describing the cultural history of this time period, but interesting to my thesis, in it Faithfull has begun her consistent use of the diction of "energy," "action," and "power." She has an instinctive understanding of the connection between physical health and energy for action. "The latter part of Queen Victoria's reign was marked by abounding activity in every department of life and thought, and an amazing output of nervous energy and original work" (3). Faithfull also points to her early life understanding of the necessity for a strong body in order to have a strong mind through the mental activity involved in "original work." Much of the change that occurred at the end of the century she accounts for as "Stored-up potential energy," and this energy converted into "explosive action, took place in every direction during the second half of the nineteenth century" (6). Even when she is at her most nationalistic, she intuits the connection of mind and body. "The Victorian days of peace abroad and respectability at home . . . also tended to the conservation of energy, and to the production of a generation amazingly strong in body and healthy in mind" (6). Virtually oblivious to the fact that the great British Empire was being secured during this time or that the country was still stinging from its incompetence during the Crimean War, Faithfull can find in those decades leading up to the end of the century, a relative calm that would produce the "original work" of the 1860s and 70s. Meanwhile, in order to mentally produce great original work, it was necessary to have great physical strength and energy.

Of course, it is in her attention to the emancipation of women that I am most interested here. "We were indeed well equipped by the inheritance of health and strength to become pioneers in every direction" (7). After this period of 'storing up energy," the time was ripe for women finally to be able to put their strong minds and bodies to use. Women could now become pioneers because they had the health and strength to do so. "The emancipation of women occurred at a time when . . . they [women] could take part in the flow of new life and thought and constructive energy" (7). To her, not only were women poised and ready to move into the public sphere intellectually, with their mental strength and ideas, but also physically with their bodies into public spaces: the workplace, the athletic gym, the university classroom, and the sports field.

In fact, "the energy that distinguished the age belongs as much to women as to men, and was forced to find new ways of manifesting itself. Like men, women wanted new worlds to explore, and the old and well-worn tracks would no longer satisfy them. They wanted a larger field for their exploits; they longed for a great adventure" (8). The outpouring of physical and mental activity by women was inevitable. They were eager to break out on "a great adventure." A "great adventure" is only possible if one is fit. These certain women of Faithfull's generation were fit. They sought the needed education to put their thoughts into action, to lead them on a "great adventure."

Not only were women like Faithfull physically prepared to gain their own authority in the world, but they also remembered women who were admirable role models: "Miss Emily Davies, Miss Clough, Miss Buss, Miss Beale, and Mrs. Garrett Anderson were splendidly strong and healthy as well as vigorous in mind" (8). These women were role models for Faithfull not only because they were in the field of education, but also because they possessed good health, physical strength, and strong minds. They were not lop-sided women of thought without strength and action nor women of strength without thought. Ultimately, Faithfull believed that these women "certainly did their part in producing the revolution in women's lives which was inevitable when girls tingling with health and strength found a world around them alight with ideas and ideals to be captured and translated into action" (9). It was inevitable. If young girls were active and encouraged to be strong in body they would naturally want to spring into action upon hearing the emancipating ideas and ideals of their age. It was not only in the form of intellectual ability and economic opportunity that Faithfull found the promise for young girls. Faithfull repeatedly attributed it to their healthy and strong bodies, an emphasis she continues throughout the entire account of her own life. By the time Faithfull sat down to commence writing her autobiography she had seen first-hand, in the examples of thousands of female students, the necessity for a strong body in order to have a sharp mind and therefore a predisposition to and the possibility of a politically active life.

Faithfull does not give a lengthy description of her childhood--just twenty pages of the almost 300-page text. Here she writes in retrospection as an adult and an educator who understands the importance of childhood on an adult's character. Yet most of the details she gives us are of the games and physical activities that she and her siblings engaged in as children. Chapter 2, "Childhood" begins with the comparison of mind and body: "How readily children's thoughts, and therefore their games, are concerned with the great events of life" (15-16). Children, who are the most essentially pure human beings, cannot help but have their thoughts and bodies connected in the form of games. What the brain thinks about the body will want to follow. Faithfull demonstrates this in her own childhood just as she will in her adult life. She understands that when young girls become educated their bodies will instinctively set out to act out those ideas.

Paper chase, hide and seek, and other games concerned "with the great events of life, birth, marriage, and death," and regular walks, games "connected in some way with the Bible," and "waiting at the table" (which they were only allowed to do if they regarded it as a game and not as an art) kept these children occupied. So important were the aspects of health and fitness of her childhood that Faithfull declared that if she were to hire a nurse for her own children "I would choose a nurse young enough in body and spirit to play with children, and enjoy on her own part a paper-chase or hide-and-seek" (16). Thus, athletic games are good not just for children but also for the female adults helping to care for them. Another important aspect of childhood that Faithfull discusses at length is diet. Intuitively she understood that "the even tenour of our days" included "regular walks, regular rests, simple meals, and occasional picnics. . . . We were told that if we were hungry we could eat what was wholesome, and might then have what was pleasant" (20-21). Balance in mind and body depend on exercise and proper nutrition. Faithfull was properly equipped to be a New Woman by her own healthy childhood. She was encouraged to be physically active and to keep her body in shape through what was even then accurately if not commonly understood to be a balanced and proper diet.

Probably the most important encouragement of the physical and competitive activities of Faithfull's childhood came from her father. She writes, "any picture of my home would be incomplete without a portrait of my father" (28). After naming where he was born, she immediately continues: "He was a lover of sport, an excellent tennis player and a moderately good golfer" (28). Of all the details about her father to name first (after his origin) she chose to name his interests in sports and fitness. His profession and relationship with her mother came second to her description of him as an athlete. Perhaps not surprisingly then, he communicated his passion for sports to his children: "He took the greatest interest in our games, and would spend a long time when he returned in the evening on instructing us in tennis, or teaching us whist, and always wanted us to understand the science of the game" (30). Nor was his enthusiasm saved only for his male children. Her father encouraged her in her activities to the point that she describes his preference in women's clothes: "He had very strong and somewhat conventional views about women's dress, and liked nothing that was not neat. A shepherd's plaid, small hat and very good shoes were what he preferred" (30). In short, he would not prefer anything that was ostentatious, or unpractical. He clearly believed female children were meant to move around comfortably and to be active.

Traditionally, athletics and sports were fine for females while children, but were then thought of as unlady-like as girls left the nursery. Yet, Faithfull's father encouraged her even while in university. At Oxford her father was interested in her athletic pursuits as much as her academic ones: "I think that perhaps he enjoyed the University tennis matches in which, though a very modest player, I represented Somerville, as much as any examination results" (30). Faithfull engaged in physical activities and competitive games throughout her university career. She described her time at Oxford: "The corporate life of the College, our societies, our games, debates and tennis matches were delightfully new and attractive. I remember the excitement of the first inter-collegiate hockey match—our disgust at the defeat of Somerville after her captain had been laid low with a black eye from someone's stick" (62). Sports and fitness were for Faithfull an essential aspect of her education, and as an adult she devoted much of her energy to advocate the same for other young women.

Throughout the early part of her autobiography, when she describes her childhood and education, Faithfull often finds opportunities to compare the educational situations of boys and girls. As a professional educator it is easy to see how she might be especially sensitive to these aspects of her childhood and her own education. As a child she had the opportunity to attend an all-boy's school run by her uncle. It was there at The Grange that she "discovered those radical differences between boys and girls in their work . . . The differences appear also in play at a very early nursery age" (40). One of the differences she notices was behavior in games. "The girl loves direction and help in all that she is doing while the small boy accepts an offer to play with him with obvious condescension and on the distinct understanding that the game is played as he wishes" (40). This notice of the chauvinism of Victorian boyhood notwithstanding, the important aspect of her comparison is that she chooses to compare the genders based on their reaction to participation in games. Faithfull's preferred setting is the classroom and her primary interest is in education, but she returns again and again to the playing field as a stage for her theory of girls' education.

She understands absolutely the importance of physical fitness and games to the girls, but is repeatedly frustrated to learn the advantages in learning opportunities that the boys have because of traditional male privilege. Describing the differences between boys and girls and the expression of their own opinions in writing essays she notes that girls write less and spend a great deal more time reading other authorities instead of relying on their own voices. "The difference" she says " is no doubt accounted for in part by the fact that boys have many other absorbing interests, which make them wish to dispose of work as quickly as possible" (40). It is only hinted at here, but the reader is made aware that if girls were allowed to choose from as many interests as the boys could then perhaps they would learn quicker to rely on their own voices. Moreover, she noticed boys could "concentrate violently for a few short minutes" and "as a rule are more accurate in remembering details." If girls were allowed so much control of their lives through the opportunity of many choices, they might also choose to heed their own voices, focus their memorization, and finish their studies more productively.

Another comparison Faithfull makes between men and women is the immense sense of desirable opportunities that women see as possibilities while studying and working with men. During her time at Oxford, she noticed that girls worked very hard with the understanding that this was a unique opportunity that they had been given. On the other hand, by the time she was out of school and had an opportunity to notice women in the workplace, she believed that women "are as apt to be unpunctual and to spend time in gossip as the men with whom they are compared. In fact, I am inclined to think that women weary sooner and find any monotony in life more insufferable than men, as, unfortunately, only too often they have not the physique which enables them to get a sufficient amount of change and recreation" (65). Moreover, even in the workplace, a woman will be better equipped if she is physically fit and is allowed opportunities to be active and maintain that fitness. Whether working in the classroom or working in the public workforce, women needed to maintain a balance between work (usually their mental life) and play (their physical life). This comparison was beneficial for women because "men were no longer debarred from women's comradeship. And if they could work together they could also play together" (63). Seeing options that were available for boys while in the classroom allowed the girls to desire similar ones. When women had the opportunity to work alongside men they soon desired to participate in the other activities, such as sports and athletics, in which they saw men participating. Women could indeed gain authority through their bodies if they were strong enough and fit enough.

Faithfull shows her understanding of physical fitness throughout her description of her childhood, through her role model father, and also through her description of a life-long friend from her days at Oxford. Her over two-page portrait of this friend is a model of the well-rounded woman. Again, like the description of her father, after one sentence

describing her family, Faithfull moves right to a description of her
physical body: "She was one of a large family and had many brothers . . .
She was built on generous lines, and body and spirit were finely matched.
She looked as if she could lead armies. Tall and handsome with the
bearing of a queen, she would have been noteworthy in any company of
women" (66). Ultimately, Faithfull found her friend's beauty to be more
than the traditional. She found her beautiful because her friend used her
body in the pleasing discipline of athletic acts. Faithfull describes her as
"radiantly alive and enjoying life. She was the best woman tennis-player
in Oxford. Underlying all was a spirit ardent with love and goodwill"
(67). This friend presents every element Faithfull offers for the well-
rounded New Woman. She must have not only high intelligence but also a
kind spirit, and it is all presented in a healthy and active body.

The remainder of Faithfull's autobiography is a combination of the
description of her career as a pioneer of education and her theories of the
type of education that girls needed: physical fitness, athletics, and games
are a necessary means for constructing compelling female personalities
who are capable of gaining power and resisting the prescription of male
authority:

> Corporate life, class-work and team games have brought wholly new
> interest into girls' lives. They have fostered and developed good
> comradeship, unselfishness, honour, courage, the power of playing a
> losing game and the qualities of leadership; and girls of to-day between the
> ages of fourteen and eighteen are healthily absorbed in both work and
> play. (46)

The emphasis here on a balance between work and athletic play is serious.
As an educator, Faithfull was keenly aware of the need for girls to have a
solid education, but this education could not be complete if these young
women were not taught to keep their bodies healthy. They needed a habit
of physical education and sports to balance their work lives. The new
interests in "class work and team games" that were being taken up in girls'
lives would be indispensible to allowing young women to see their
potential as emancipated women. Those interests were now being taken
up, but in order for young women to have authority in the public sphere
they must develop, among other qualities, "the power of playing a losing
game." Poise in losing in physical competition provides the basis for
endurance and balance in intellectual form. There are certain personal
qualities that are simply more adequately developed during the playing of
sports and games.

By chapter 5 in her autobiography, Faithfull has finished at Oxford and is trying to find employment. She received her first post as a teacher at the Oxford High School. "It was one of the schools belonging to the Girls' Public Day School Trust" (75). While there, she saw the deplorable state of their athletic grounds, she noted that always when a school lacked an endowment, it was also missing important equipment. Faithfull defined important equipment as "Laboratories, playing fields, gymnasiums, and swimming baths" (76). These should not be extras or extra privileges of students. They were necessary to a girl's education. At this point in the telling of her life story Faithfull comments on the success of high schools at the time. "Lessons were short and the time-table so arranged as to give variety and avoid fatigue, and a girl's physical, mental and moral characteristics were studied by their teachers as never before" (78). If a new generation of women were to challenge the politics of the day, challenge the existing codes of public employment, or have a life different than her mother's her physical well-being must be completely exercised: "High schools had no playgrounds in those days. The founders of the movement had failed to see this necessity for their schools and did not provide sufficiently for physical development" (78). Again, Faithfull believed that in order for a girl to be a strong student, and therefore a strong woman, a woman with authority in public, schools had to make provisions in their schedules and had adequate equipment and space for playing fields.

Because of this, when she arrived at her second teaching position at The Royal Holloway College, one of the first things that she noticed was the expansive grounds:

> Games were, however, the chief distraction, and the provision made for them was as excellent as it was meager and poor in the High Schools. The ninety-five acres belonging to the college gave every opportunity for tennis and hockey, and at these, also, the staff joined the students. There was a swimming bath and a gymnasium, but in the summer term the river was the chief delight. (94)

The students could have been diverted from their studies by taking breaks going to parties or other social gatherings that were often held. The young women could have taken breaks by having elaborate tea parties to divert them from their studies or by retreating to their rooms in solitude or for reading, sewing, and piano playing. Instead, she remembers that it was sports that were the primary choice of the young women when needing a break from their work. Moreover, the staff often joined the students in their sports. There was much for a student to learn on the fields that could

34

not be learned in the classroom. At the same time, there was much a teacher could learn about a student during these important learning moments. If there were no sports, "there was also the disadvantage that the teacher met her class only in the classroom" (79). Much of a young woman's personality could be seen in no other way than on the playing field as she participated in sports. Furthermore, a teacher could encourage a young woman to be more aggressive in the classroom by seeing how she reacted in a competitive situation. The energy and competitiveness and emergence of an authority of a public personality on the playing field cannot be duplicated in the classroom.

As Faithfull's New Woman is guided through health and fitness to the authorship of a maturing self, she is always cautioned not to make athletics the primary goal of education. Faithfull tells the story of a parent who complained that:

> athletics were occupying too much large a place in the life and affections of the girls. A parent brought a girl of seventeen to me with the pathetic appeal: "I hope you will try to make her care for books. She went to school with a taste for literature and returned with nothing but a taste for hockey." It was complained by many that a place in the hockey XI was far more coveted by a girl than a high place in her form, and that this was recognized and hardly discouraged by the authorities. In this, as in all other matters, it is difficult to keep an even balance. (79)

Yet, keeping a balance was always the goal. Whether it was sports for the young women in high school or athletics for the staff, Faithfull was determined that the female body must be attended to in the same way male bodies had been for centuries. She was convinced it would be impossible for girls to have a high level of success in a public life if they were not physically fit. Not only did the students need fitness to enable their best intelligence but she instinctively knew that self-esteem and personal authority could certainly be gained through participation in sports and athletics. Faithfull in this way was a pioneer. She anticipated by some 100 years the 1995 Nike sports company ad campaign that has encouraged girls' participation in sports by naming all that their participation could do for them. "If you let me play sports, I will like myself more. I will have more self-confidence. I will be more likely to leave a man who beats me. I will be 60% less likely to get breast cancer."[7] In 1995 Nike used the same argument that Lillian Faithfull used in her autobiography. Personal authority and public agency can be gained for young women if they are allowed to play sports and to be physically active.

In 1894 Faithfull took a position as Vice-Principal for the Ladies' Department of King's College in Kensington Square. This was a non-residential college and one of Faithfull's immediate concerns was to compare residential education with non-residential education. Of course, because fitness was so important to her and to her ideas of women's education she deplores the lack of games at a non-residential college: "A non-resident College needs corporate games and societies greatly, and all these should be organized by the students themselves" (114). Students at a residential college would have games organized for them as part of the program of their school. At a non-residential college this would be missing. Students and staff alike could always "board an omnibus with the rest of the Hockey Eleven and play in mud and fog" (114). In order to maintain the balance between work and play that she prescribes throughout, the women must be encouraged to organize activities for themselves while they were away from the campus.

Faithfull remained at King's College until 1906 when she took over the position of head principal of Cheltenham Ladies College from Dorothea Beale, its founder. While there, the students, after learning she had been made President of the All England Women's Hockey Association, "were disappointed that my [her] time and attention were not more exclusively devoted to athletics" (134). This is the first mention that she makes of her nomination to that position. Athletics for her were not only a matter of importance for her students but also for her personal culture. She would not have been the professionally effective administrator that she was without her lifetime investment in athletics. It was this investment that she encouraged in her students. She was energetically focused on the health of the bodies of her students. Shortly after she arrived at Cheltenham she began an annual medical inspection. It was among the initiatives that made the town suspicious of this new principal.

> A letter appeared in the local press condemning the fads of the new Principal in introducing annual medical inspections for the College girls, and signed 'One of the unfaithful.' It was not long, however, before the value of this annual inspection in maintaining a high standard of health among the pupils was generally recognized. It also provided a valuable body of statistics, probably unparalleled, concerning the health of a large secondary school. (142)

The pun on Faithfull's name aside, the results convinced the community of the value of the health plan for the students. Women could gain authority through education, but this education could not be acquired nor used by women who were not physically fit. Authority could only be present in a healthy body.

Her advocacy was successful. "The college record of health was so good that it should have done much to dispel all fears as to the Cheltenham climate. Again and again the Medical Inspector commented upon the physique of the girls and their vigorous health" (149). Despite the reputation of unhealthy weather to be found in Cheltenham, she was able to keep her students healthy. Faithfull notes, "I do not think that normal children of school age are very susceptible to climate, and the healthy conditions of their regular life, wholesome food, airy room, and plenty of exercise in games and gymnasium, more than compensate for a place being relaxing" (149). Though the surroundings of Cheltenham were less than normally comfortable, her students stayed healthy. Wholesome food and plenty of exercise will not stress a woman but make her stronger.

Near the end of the autobiography is a chapter to recollect all that she has learned about the education of girls and women. She declares, "in the course of forty years I believe that I have gained a knowledge of children, girls and women, between the ages of five and twenty-five" (195-6). She emphasizes physical fitness and athletics equally with cognitive development and mental activism. "I have watched their physical, intellectual, social, moral, and religious development. I have been their comrade, teacher, director in studies and games, and their counselor in the conduct of their lives" (196). In her role as educational expert and accomplished amateur athlete she had watched for forty years the development of girls into young women. After all of that experience Faithfull offers her final prescription as to the best type of student: "It is the healthy girl—healthy in mind and body, with plenty of vigour and energy—who makes the greatest impression upon one, for she calls out one's vitality; and when teaching a class one finds oneself unconsciously addressing her" (197). The girl who is physically active and healthy will have cognitive poise and authoritative agency. The New Woman was a woman who would not be ignored. Faithfull, and her students, had this quality.

Moreover, Faithfull is careful to notice that many students fall prey to the complaint that athletic girls are too aggressive. She rebuts that instead by pointing out the good that comes from aggressive tendencies.

> Self-sufficiency and aggressiveness are charges often brought against girls nowadays, but these are not apparent in their ordinary life. If they are trained to take responsibility in small ways, and taught to rule not only themselves but groups of their companions, it is, of course, natural that they should develop an assurance not to be found in girls entirely brought up at home, nor in girls of an earlier generation. (199)

Aggressiveness is a personality trait almost indispensable on the playing fields. To Faithfull, unlike many of her contemporaries who assumed that serious education for girls might make them unwomanly, aggressiveness is a positive trait. Of course, just such aggressiveness was to be characteristic of a new type of female person no longer principally interested in domestic life or even in marriage. Competitiveness and skill in games were so important that Faithfull instituted a grading system that began when girls entered the school:

> I instituted the same system of grading in games, and it proved to be an unqualified success. It seemed to me that the first and second College and House Elevens absorbed the attention of the games mistresses too much, to the exclusion of the training of the rank and file. We wanted a general interest to be encouraged, and the general standard of play to be raised throughout the College. It was most important that every girl should receive careful instruction in the science of the various games and be prevented from getting into bad habits. The players were therefore graded on entering College, so that those of the same standard of knowledge and capacity played together and were coached together. Special care was taken with the training of the younger children, and the Junior grade was entrusted to the most expert teacher. By the end of the first session such good material had been found among the Juniors and such rapid progress made by them, that there was some competition among the coaches for the pleasure of teaching them. (138)

In this extraordinary passage, several of Faithfull's beliefs are evident. Playing hockey is important enough that everyone in the school should be encouraged to play and to play well. All girls "of the rank and file" needed careful instruction to "keep from getting into bad habits." In order for girls to be good at hockey they must practice and, in addition, practice proper technique with a coach. The same principal of practicing writing in a classroom or working on mathematics problems held true on the field. Moreover, this type of athletic instruction is just as important and therefore deserves the same system of grading. Faithfull, almost in passing, makes the revolutionary statement, "We wanted the general standard of play to be raised throughout the college." Why does the entire college need to be good hockey players? Why shouldn't just the women participating on the hockey team have to be aggressive and capable players? The answer is that she hoped to inspire emancipated activist women. So the entire school should be good hockey players.

Faithfull ends her autobiography by describing how she believes a professional educator should act: "It is not only good for the school mistress to be an athlete, it is good [also] that she should be with the girls on the playing fields" (206). A successful teacher must be an athlete, and as a role model, she would demonstrate this to her students. A woman's body in Faithfull's text is an instrument of subversive practice in pursuit of the political emancipation of the subject. As she envisions the prospects of her students, Faithfull does not believe at all that women should receive an education to make them better wives. Instead she writes, "Surely the right course for a woman, as for a man, is to enter the profession for which she is best fitted, paid or unpaid" (270). To fashion the politically precocious female personality that is comfortable with herself she advises, in a chapter called "Professional Life," "To have touch of politics, art, music and literature; to be keenly interested in problems of all kinds; to travel, and to have some form of athletics, is to prevent oneself from becoming a very dull dog" (263). As she defines a professional woman's adult life, she values a place in it for athletics. After women are out of school, their bodies continue to need health and action to keep themselves "fit" for the work of their professional life. Later she writes of "the obvious gain of some sort of athletics to all working women" (266). By this point in her autobiography, she assumes that the necessity of athletics to every woman should be obvious. It is necessary to have a physically graceful body in order to possess authority. Such grace is the natural acquisition of the athlete.

More than anything else, Faithfull's autobiography is an example of a too long overlooked body of evidence of *fin de siècle* women—New Women in particular—who would subvert traditional patriarchal cultural authority by encouraging women in their girlhood to imagine a maturity that always combines intellectual pursuits, physical fitness, and athletics. In writing her story, Faithfull offers a persistent narrative for other women. She created, as did other New Women autobiographers a "new female subject" (15). Faithfull emphasizes in her autobiography that her remarkable life was owed in large part to her physical and athletic abilities. She is a remarkable New Woman because not only does she write an autobiography that notices these characteristics in herself, but also as a pioneering educator she offers these qualities as a prescription for the creation of a next generation of women. Women like Faithfull chose to write life stories that not only brought attention to their athletic culture, but also explicitly named and assigned the ways that their bodies could be used and would be used as agents and authors of change and emancipation.

Works cited

Bell, Susan Groag and Marilyn Yalom.   Eds.   *Revealing Lives: Autobiography, Biography, and Gender*. New York: State Univ. of New York P, 1990.

Benstock, Shari. "Authorizing the Autobiographical." In *The Private Self: Theory and Practices of Women's Autobiographical Writings*. Shari Benstock Ed. Chapel Hill: Univ. of North Carolina P, 1988.

Beauvoir, Simone. *The Second Self*. Trans. H. M. Parshley. New York: Knopf, 1952.

Butler, Judith. *Gender Trouble: Feminism and the Subversion of Identity*. New York: Routledge, 1990.

Castelnuovo, Shirley and Sharon Guthrie.   *Feminism and the Female Body: Liberating the Amazon Within*.   London: Lynne Rienner Publishers, 1998.

Corbett, Mary Jean. *Representing Femininity: Middle Class Subjectivity in Victorian and Edwardian Women's Autobiographies*.   Oxford: Oxford UP, 1992.

Danahay, Martin A. *A Community of One: Masculine Autobiography and Autonomy in Nineteenth-Century Britain*.   New York: State U of NewYork P, 1993.

"The Definitions of Self and Form in Feminist Autobiography Theory".

Faithfull, Lillian M. *In the House of My Pilgrimage*. London: Chatto and Windus, 1925.

Gagnier, Regenia.   *Subjectivities: A History of Self-Representation in Britain, 1832-1920*. Oxford: Oxford UP, 1991.

Goozé, Marjanne Elaine. "The Definitions of Self and Form in Feminist Autobiography Theory." *Women's Studies: An Interdisciplinary Journal* 21 (1992): 411-429.

Jelinek, Estelle C.   *The Tradition of Women's Autobiography: From Antiquity to the Present*. Boston: Twayne Publishers, 1986.

—.   Ed. *Women's Autobiography: Essays in Criticism*. Bloomington: Indiana UP, 1980.

Lejeune, Philippe. *On Autobiography*.   Trans. by Paul John Eakin. Minneapolis, MN: Univ. of Minnesota Press, 1988.

Marcus, Laura.   *Auto/biographical Discourses: Theory, Criticism, Practice*. Manchester, Manchester UP, 1994.

Neuman, Shirley.   "Autobiography and Questions of Gender: An Introduction" in *Autobiography and Questions of Gender*.   Shirley Neuman Ed. London: Cass, 1991.

Olney, James. "Autobiography and the Cultural Moment: A Thematic, Historical, and Bibliographical Introduction." *Autobiography: Essays Theoretical and Critical.* Ed. James Olney. Princeton: Princeton UP, 1980.

Peterson, Linda. *Traditions of Victorian Women's Autobiography: The Poetics and Politics of Life Writing* Charlottesville, UP of Virginia, 1999.

Smith, Sidonie and Julia Watson. "Introduction: Situating Subjectivity in Women's Autobiographical Practices" in *Women, Autobiography, Theory: A Reader.* Smith and Watson Eds. Madison, WI, Univ. of Wisconsin Press, 1988.

Spengemann, William. *The Forms of Autobiography: Episodes in the History of a Literary Genre.* New Haven, CT: Yale UP, 1980.

Stanton, Domna. "Is the Subject Different?" *The Female Autograph: Theory and Practice of Autobiography from the Tenth to the Twentieth Century.* Ed. by Domna Stanton. New York: New York Literary Forum, 1984.

Watson, Martha. *Lives of Their Own: Rhetorical Dimensions in Autobiographies of Women Activists.* Columbia, SC: Univ. of South Carolina P, 1999.

Notes

[1] I am indebted here to the following texts for their various studies of autobiography: "Autobiography and the Cultural Moment" by James Olney in *Autobiography: Essays Theoretical and Critical* (1980); "Introduction: Situating Subjectivity in Women's Autobiographical Practices" by Sidonie Smith and Julia Watson in *Women, Autobiography, Theory: A Reader* (1998); "Authorizing the Autobiographical" by Shari Benstock in *The Private Self: Theory and Practice of Women's Autobiographical Writings* (1988); "The Definitions of Self and Form in Feminist Autobiography Theory" in *Women's Studies,* 21: (1992), and "Autobiography and Questions of Gender: An Introduction" by Shirley Neuman in *Autobiography and Questions of Gender* (1991).

[2] See Philippe Lejeune's *On Autobiography* (1988), Martin Danahay''s *A Community of One: Masculine Autobiography and Autonomy in Nineteenth-Century Britain* (1993), William Spengemann's *The Forms of Autobiography: Episodes in the History of a Literary Genre* (1980), and Martha Watsons's *Lives of Their Own: Rhetorical Dimensions in Autobiographies of Women Activists* (1999) for a more detailed discussion of the "autobiographical I" and the pact between the author of autobiography and the reader of this genre.

[3] Other critics have also resisted this disposition to define a tradition based solely on gender. Reginia Gagnier in *Subjectivities* focuses on the texts of working-class women and men by analyzing "how subjects see themselves in response to the material and cultural 'facts' of their lives" (11). Also Laura Marcus in *Auto/biographical Discourses: Theory, Criticism, Practice* (1994) questions a women's tradition by charting the diversity of discourse about autobiographical genres in the nineteenth century. Peterson and Marcus are both more interested in noticing the ways in which a literary history for autobiography was constructed in the Victorian period. It would be gender inclusive, of course.

[4] For a complete history of "bodies and desire" see the introduction to *Women, Autobiography, Theory: A Reader* (1992) by Sidonie Smith and Julia Watson, and it is to that introduction that I am indebted for the immediately following commentary.

[5] More on the naming of the female body as "other" is in Simone de Beauvoir's *The Second Sex* (1952) and Judith Butler's *Gender Trouble: Feminism and the Subversion of Identity* (1990).

[6] These two elements of the sporting New Woman are assembled and analyzed in a larger study I have undertaken.

[7] This 1995 commercial developed by the Wieden and Kennedy Agency of Portland, Oregon can be viewed at *www.youtube.com/watch?v=AQ_XSHpIbZE*

CHAPTER THREE

OF 'OLOGIES AND 'ISMS:
MONA CAIRD REWRITING AUTHORITY

ABIGAIL MANN

In an 1895 article in *Blackwood's Magazine* Hugo Stutfield satirized the typical New Woman, "with her head full of all the 'ologies and 'isms, with sex-problems and heredity, and other gleanings from the surgery and the lecture-room" (238). Stutfield's description evidences the discomfort many felt as the New Woman ventured into previously "unfeminine" scientific fields, particularly those dealing with the evolutionary concerns of "sex-problems and heredity." Notable New Women such as Mona Caird and Sarah Grand explicitly referenced Darwin in their work, and the influence of evolutionary ideas permeated New Woman discourse at almost every level. For instance, an 1889 exchange in *Nineteenth Century* centered on women's suffrage invokes a dizzying array of evolutionary motifs within the space of about twelve pages: the changing conditions to which women are subjected, the "battle of life" in which women are engaged, the fact that change is not sweeping but takes place in slow steps, and ideas about speciation and degeneration all appear in the arguments for women's rights (Fawcett 126; Dilke 134). Well might Stutfield attempt to defuse the rhetorical power of such approaches by suggesting that the New Woman's affiliation with evolutionary discourse amounted to nothing more than a parrot-like "gleaning" of terms and scraps of information.

This article posits that for certain New Woman evolutionary thought consisted of more than simply another "'olog[y or] 'ism" to be referenced to prove intellectual fitness. These New Women did not simply echo the language of learned scientists. Instead, evolutionary ideas acted as a catalyst, giving these women authority to ask Darwinian questions in order to offer up alternate readings of old debates about control over the female body.[1] In other words, such writers were, as much as men like Alfred Russel Wallace and T.H. Huxley, co-theorists of evolution who examined the social and ethical possibilities it engendered. The work of Mona Caird

(1854?-1932) reveals a complex, but sustained, commitment to Darwinian ideas. More than rhetorical flourish, certain patterns of evolutionary thought, particularly keen attention to the tropes of interaction and indeterminacy, shape both her non-fiction and fiction. In keeping with the theme of this collection, I argue that Caird's ability to both work with evolutionary ideas and yet differ significantly from the dominant discourse built around Darwinism offers an alternate model of a New Woman approach to authority, one that seeks to combine multiple discourses rather than simply replace any one authoritative voice. It is not coincidental that evolutionary thought, a discourse focused on the interactions of material bodies, offers a space for Caird to rewrite authority, particularly authority that attempted to dictate women's relations to their own bodies. Caird treats language like an evolutionary body: rather than seeing the dominant discourse as one which the rebel must ever struggle against or wearily accede to, she traces the ways that interactions between seemingly set authorities can, like the actions of natural selection, lead to unpredictable new configurations of both language and bodies.

I begin this reading with a brief examination of some of Caird's nonfictional writings. Their rhetoric not only consistently valorizes evolutionary thought, but, in both content and form, highlights both the interaction and the indeterminacy that Caird found so useful in evolutionary thinking. I then turn to 1894's *The Daughters of Danaus*, in which the story of Professor Fortescue, a scientific hero whose wife cannot evolve to her full potential, demonstrates the pitfalls of ignoring these qualities. Caird uses evolutionary ideas to rework the idea of single voiced authority. Embracing the interaction between discourses offered a new way out of old dilemmas for the New Woman, who struggled against authoritative pronouncements about the capabilities and functions of their own bodies, particularly in regards to motherhood. Critics have almost unanimously read *Daughters's* heroine, Hadria's, attempts to redefine her relationship to maternity as futile, but though her experiments in alternative mothering do ultimately fail, I argue that they succeed at forcing new conversations and narratives, and thus opening up the possibility of change. Caird's writing indicates that understanding women as evolutionary bodies and tracing how they are shaped by interaction, both physical and rhetorical, begins to shape a better future for both the individual and the species.

What exactly did evolutionary thought mean to Caird? By the end of the century Darwinism could be understood to reference anything from abundance to extinction, from hereditary determination to chance and indeterminacy. Indeed, this abundance of applications justifies why I use

"Darwinian," "Darwinism" and "evolutionary" almost interchangeably as descriptors of the ideas Caird (and many other New Woman writers) engaged with; while the publication of *The Origin* certainly fueled interest in and acceptance of ideas about evolution, many of these concepts were discussed well before Darwin's work, and the various manifestations in which these concepts appeared after *The Origin's* publication certainly stray far from Darwin's intended use.[2]

Caird was specifically familiar with Darwin's writings, evidenced through her association with Karl Pearson's Men and Women's Club. As this extract from the end of *The Origin* demonstrates, Darwin regularly conflated language and evolutionary forces.[3] Summing up the actions of natural selection, Darwin writes that

> I look at the natural geological record, as a history of the world imperfectly kept, and written in a changing dialect…only here and there a short chapter has been preserved; and of each page, only here and there a few lines. Each word of the slowly-changing language, in which the history is supposed to be written, being more or less different in the interrupted succession of chapters, may represent the apparently abruptly changed forms of life, entombed in our consecutive, but widely separated formations. (310)

While Darwin primarily sought to justify the lack of continuous forms here, this passage stresses the interaction between seemingly unrelated forms, or "dialects," as well as the unpredictability of "apparently abrupt" change. These concepts structured Caird's work conceptually and formally, and allowed her to suggest a more evolutionary approach to social change, one based on the modifications wrought by interacting bodies and discourses.

Caird consistently treats discourse as an evolutionary body, forcing it to interact with new ideas and tracing the unpredictable new configurations that result. Drawing upon Mikhail Bahktin's narrative theory, as well as the close affinity Darwin himself posited between language and species, I term this formal technique Darwinian dialogism: texts shape and change each other through their interactions, disrupting authoritative narratives, just as organisms in evolutionary theory constantly change due to their interaction with each other.[4] Caird does not simply create an environment of interacting texts, she also suggests that these interactions may bring forth previously unrecognized elements, just as natural selection may work upon seemingly insignificant variations. In *The Origin,* Darwin uses a desert island as a metaphor to explain the power of natural selection. While the barriers would create a land "into which new and, better adapted forms could not freely enter," if those barriers were breached,

> every slight modification, which in the course of ages chanced to arise, and which in any way favoured the individuals of any of the species, by better adapting them to their altered conditions, would tend to be preserved; and natural selection would thus have free scope for the work of improvement. (81-2)

These differences may be "slight," but they are crucial; in a new environment, forced to interact with others (be they organisms or texts), a small difference or aspect, "in any way favour[able]" may take on great importance.

While Bahktin's work focuses on novelistic heteroglossia, he argues that in conjunction with the nineteenth- century ascendency of the novel, all genres become "novelized"; "the novelization of the other genres does not imply their subjection to an alien genric canon," he writes, but rather stresses the way that they are opened up to multiple meanings so that "novelization implies their liberation from all that serves as a brake in their unique development" (63). Without getting into a complicated untangling of origin and influence, I think it is fair to say that Caird found evolutionary ideas a powerful catalyst in creating a heteroglossic subversiveness that played out most fully within her novels. In her nonfiction, Caird stresses that no text carries stable meaning, but instead adapts itself to differing uses and shapes.[5] She forces language to act as an evolutionary body, shaping and shaped by that which surrounds it rather than forever stable.

Caird entered the public stage in 1888 with her article "Marriage," which traces the history of matrimony from an evolutionary perspective. In its final lines, Caird triumphantly declares that

> evolution has ceased to be a power driving us like dead leaves on a gale; thanks to science, we are no longer entirely blind, and we aspire to direct that mighty force for the good of humanity. We see a limitless field of possibility opening out before us; the adventurous spirit might leap up at the wonderful romance of life! (198)

She seemingly valorizes the authoritative narrative of science as one that can replace older, more restrictive narratives. In a contemporaneous article entitled "Science and the Rights of Women," H.E. Harvey explicitly paints science as a competing and preferable narrative about female history, arguing that "literature tells us that man was created first, and that woman was made as an afterthought, in order to be a companion to him. But science knows nothing of this tale" (168). Unlike writers such as Harvey, however, Caird does not just trust in the "tales" of science: her Darwinian dialogism consistently highlights productive interaction and indeterminacy between competing tales.[6]

Interaction serves as a key element to Darwinian natural selection, ever alert to the "conditions of life," and built upon an organism's "infinitely complex relations to other organic beings and to external nature" (*Origin* 5, 61).[7] Even within the teleological exhortation above, Caird emphasizes that humans and evolution must work together: the newly sighted observer can "aspire to direct," but Caird remains highly aware of the power and "might" of evolution. Interaction can hardly be called an exclusively evolutionary trope, but a marked number of New Women certainly emphasized the Darwinian argument that interaction between organisms necessarily led to change, as seen in M.M. Dilke's statement that the "increased order and propriety of English life" necessarily caused women, as well as men, to evolve (133). For those New Woman who used it, the trope of interaction promised that change in one element necessarily enacted change in other, seemingly stable, structures and systems: if the British public wants to tout its progress, it has to accept that women, as well as men, would advance.

Caird pairs her emphasis on interaction with a scientific approach marked by rigorous examination of shifting conditions, exemplified by statements such as "anyone who has observed carefully knows how grateful a response the human organism gives to improved conditions, if only those remain constant" ("Marriage" 197-8). Interaction also becomes a formal principle rather than simply a rhetorical flourish. The excessive footnotes in the anti-vivisection text, "The Sanctuary of Mercy" physically demonstrate this. The footnotes often take up more than half of each page, interrupting the shape of Caird's own text as well as the original cited texts (which, broken up by Caird's own commentary and other sources, are strung across multiple pages and physically pile upon each other). This Darwinian dialogism reshapes the original narratives, adapting them to new uses. By consistently interrupting her own argument through footnotes, Caird encourages the reader, who acts in the role of a scientific observer, to literally piece together her points.[8] Both the content, which conjoins seemingly disparate texts, and the appearance of the text, which constantly interrupts itself, suggest that there is no one authoritative text, but rather an amalgam of various texts whose meanings shape and reshape each other.

Caird applied the indeterminacy fueled by interaction to narratives about social structures, particularly those that seemed to be authorized by science, but were actually open to revision and evolution.[9] For Darwin, interaction between organisms and environment resulted in indeterminacy as to the final outcome of that contact. Late in *The Origin*, he describes natural selection as "the accumulation of innumerable slight variations, each good for the individual possessor," but unexpected in its final configuration (459). In "Marriage," Caird argues that the nature of woman must be understood as part of the same scheme, protesting

> against the exclusion of the ideas of evolution, of natural selection, of the well known influence upon organs and aptitudes of continued use or disuse, influence…which is freely acknowledged in the discussion of all questions except those in which woman forms an important element. "As she was in the beginning, is now and ever shall be—!" (185)

Insisting upon the indeterminacy impelled by interacting, "influencing" elements, Caird did not seek some sort of post-Derridian free for all, but rather a flexible narrative which, with each interaction, would subtly adapt to the conditions of the user. She suggests that if, rather than accepting science as an authoritative voice, commentators can come to understand it as one that forces an understanding of "apparently limitless adaptability," as she states later in the article (185), language and bodies can interact in more fruitful ways. The seemingly fixed nature of female character actually turns out to be in flux—by understanding women as bodies, Caird argues, her Darwinian dialogism breaks down the authority to fix the meaning of those bodies, but also gain a new authority to encourage different configurations.

The authority of science, in interaction with the rhetoric of the women's movement, catalyzed new narratives about women, and new possibilities for the actual interactions of women's bodies within such narratives. In her recent *Feminist Realism at the Fin de Siecle,* Molly Youngkin argues that New Woman realism depended on both new rhetoric and new material conditions: successful New Woman realism required "a transformation of *consciousness* to realize their condition, articulate[ion of] their condition through *spoken word*, and use [of] *concrete action* to change their condition" (7). Caird's employment of Darwinian ideas and techniques catalyzing social change in *The Daughters of Danaus* offers a model of achieving these crucial New Woman goals by re-envisioning the formation and power of authoritative discourses and insisting upon their relation to interacting bodies.

Daughters might be summed up briefly as "independent woman marries a conventional man, is unhappy, leaves him and their children to try to make it as a musician, starts to succeed but is called back by her mother's illness, and ends up bowing to familial and social pressures." For this reason, most critics have read the novel as a failure: while Hadria tries to change, she ultimately does not succeed in her attempts. I certainly don't want to argue that this is a happy novel (although in comparison to the suicides and madness that haunt many of Caird's others novels, it has a certain cheeriness), but I do find it more hopeful than most critics acknowledge. While no great change occurs in the novel, there are some small changes in attitudes and understanding that suggest a possibility for further change in the future. In linking narrative and bodies, Caird inhabits an important lesson of Darwinian evolution: "Natura non facit saltum" (471). Nature does not make leaps: the evolutionary activist must expect a long struggle with many dead-ends. In *Daughters* Caird's interest in evolutionary thoughts manifests formally, through Darwinian dialogism between characters; thematically, in terms of the focus on women's roles in life, particularly in terms of maternity and self-sacrifice (here the formal interest in dialogism also plays a key role as the characters cycle through seemingly endless iterations of the same discussions that actually get modified in each iteration and thus lose their seemingly untouchable authority); and socially in terms of modeling a long-term and often frustrating road to change.

When Hadria Fullerton first meets her future husband, Hubert Temperley, he immediately positions himself according to evolutionary discourse. Entering into a debate about the role of natural selection in human history, Temperley declares that

> a vast deal of nonsense is talked in the name of philosophy...People seem to think that they have only to quote Spencer or Huxley, or take an interest in heredity, to justify themselves in throwing off all the trammels, as they would regard them, of duty and common sense. (77)

While Temperley is far from the hero of the text, the reader is asked to take seriously his indictment of "Spencer or Huxley" and other evolutionary thinkers. Throughout the novel, Caird suggests that references to evolutionary thinkers have replaced reasoned arguments and feasible models of change. Caird does not dismiss the "limitless field of possibility" she sees evolution offering up in "Marriage" (198). She does, however, suggest that even the most right-minded characters can defeat their own purposes by believing that creating a new narrative affects immediate and broad scale change. In an 1892 article, Caird declared her refusal to reduce debate to the "simple school-room form of discussion, consisting in flat contradiction, persistently repeated until the energies give out" ("Defence" 811). This attitude was aimed at those with whom she was socially and politically simpatico, as well as the more conservative thinkers who argued against her. Evolutionary ideas offered a valid model of and possibility for change, Caird argues, because they emphasized that change required interaction and was ultimately unpredictable. *Daughters* valorizes Darwinian dialogism, but remains acutely aware of the pitfalls of painting it as a savior that will allow immediate escape from the "trammels…of duty and common sense."

Thus while Professor Fortescue is minor in terms of the text's plot, I read him as emblematic of the complications of relying too much upon the authority of science. Not merely the text's spokesperson for evolution as a positive force, Caird paints Fortescue as the *product* of evolution at its finest:

> he had gone many steps farther in that direction than the rest of his generation. He was dowered with instincts and perceptions belonging to some kinder, nobler race than ours. (100)[10]

The Professor does serve as a vehicle for a great deal of scientific discussion, and Caird uses him to introduce and demonstrate a number of scientific beliefs that she herself holds. But as exciting and fruitful as Caird finds the ideas of evolution, they require interaction. Caird dwells on Fortescue because, despite his proper understanding of both science and politics, he corresponds to Temperley's subject who thinks he needs "only to quote Spencer or Huxley" to effect social change. The Professor cannot rescue anyone because he acts as a solo mouthpiece rather than an interactive being rooted in the material world and its realities. By placing this fault in the mouth of a scientist, Caird demonstrates how very seductive, yet ultimately dangerous, it can be to build evolutionary stories without material details. This tendency can be most clearly seen in the life and suicide of Fortescue's wife.

As a Darwinian spokesperson, Fortescue displays both a nuanced understanding of the conditions that shaped his wife, Eleanor, and a knowledgeable stance in regards to the ways such an inheritance shapes an individual. Eleanor came from a line of "violent and tyrannical" men who attracted women who "made a virtue of submitting to tyranny, and even to downright cruelty." He claims that in the end, "these poor unselfish women, piling up their own supposed merit, at the expense of the character of their tyrants, laid up a store of misery for their descendant, my unhappy wife" (203). While his description falls into a long established discourse about heredity, the professor's position as the spokesman of evolutionary ideas in the text suggests that he is viewing Eleanor's history with a Darwinian eye, focusing on how the "conditions" of tyranny and interactions between husbands and wives shaped the women of Eleanor's line (an argument very similar to that Caird presented in "Marriage").

But a significant problem arises as the professor tells his tale: an over-reliance on the authority of one narrative to change actual bodies. The professor anticipates change, but too naively trusts that understanding the past will change the future in predictable ways. He envisions watching his wife gradually evolve:

> I saw that a great development was before her. I pleased myself with the thought of watching and helping it. She was built on a grand scale. To set her free from prejudice, from her injustice to herself, from her dependence on me, to teach her to breathe deep with those big lungs of hers and think bravely with that capacious brain: that was my dream. (201)

"Great development" is a grand rhetorical flourish, but does not account for what interactions will take place and what actual shifts will occur. The Professor reads Elinor's body—"those big lungs of her" and "that capacious brain"—as under his narrative control, objects that he can "dream" into productivity. Because Fortescue invests in a broad narrative without attending to the required details (the painful, slow minutiae of evolution), what might have been a viable hope for change cannot come to fruition. Rather than understanding social evolution as a "desperate civil war" (204), in which real bodies interact with various conditions, the professor views Eleanor's evolution as an individual tale, understood expressly by him. In doing so, he transforms evolutionary theory—which Caird embraces precisely because it embodies a malleable discourse necessarily shaped by multiple influences—into a monologic and unvarying narrative. Elinor's suicide stands witness to both the evolutionary indeterminacy in transforming bodies and the hopelessness of changing bodies by relying on replacing, rather than altering, authority.

Caird embraces the narrative potential of biology, which allows people to picture new and freeing futures, but she stresses the need for conscious narrativization.[11] The activism she posits consists of more than telling a story of how evolution *ought* to occur; Darwinian dialogism requires awareness of the multiple discourses in play and alertness to how interaction reshapes them.[12] While sympathetic, Fortescue is ultimately dangerous because he seeks a science that shuts down, rather than opens, alternate paths. This example demonstrates the complicated position Caird takes up vis-à-vis Darwinian thought. The professor's evolutionary argument "that Nature offers a large choice to humanity, for the developing, balancing, annulling of its various forces of good and evil" represents a truthful and optimistic philosophy (95). But simply recognizing flexibility does not guarantee change.

In her discussion of motherhood, Caird takes on a discourse specifically about female bodies and particularly subject to authoritative pronouncements and subjects it to Darwinian dialogism. Women, the text suggests, too often avoid discussion about the variety of forms motherhood might take. "Though our well-brought-up girls shrink from…frank speech" about the nature of maternity, Hadria notes, "they don't mind playing the part of cows so long as one doesn't mention it" (172). Along with a handful of New Woman writers, including Victoria Cross and Sara Jeanette Duncan, Caird questioned the biological fixity of maternal instinct.[13] Yet her Darwinian dialogism demanded that both sides of the issue be aired, and that women do understand that, while not "cows," they are indeed bodies subject to instinct.

I end this chapter examining Hadria's actual maternal experiments— she leaves her own children in the care of her sister in law while she goes to Paris to become a musician and takes the illegitimate child of a dead school-teacher along with her to raise on her own— and how they model, as Youngkin terms it, "concrete action." But these experiments take shape in an atmosphere of constant discussions that reiterate and challenge authoritative takes on the nature of motherhood. Without an understanding the importance of, and progress made in, this framework, the actual action Hadria takes loses the significance it actually bears. The climax of the text features an extended discussion between Hadria and her conservative sister-in-law, Henriette. While the conversation allows Hadria's fullest pronouncement of her vision of motherhood, the text suggests that her manifesto requires interaction with Henriette, who serves as the authoritative voice of tradition. The interaction reshapes Hadria's own understanding of her bodily relation to motherhood. Early in the text, she suggests that scientific authority seeks to fix maternity, noting that "if we venture to hint that this unsatisfactory skeleton may be modified in form, science becomes stern" (257). By referencing a skeleton, the most material evidence Darwin offers up to support the existence of natural selection, Caird stresses that women are indeed evolutionary bodies that are subject to "modification."

Through emphasizing the materiality of mothering in the latter part of the text, Hadria alters its parameters. In Paris, as Henriette tries to convince Hadria to return home, each woman shifts slightly in her views. Henriette's language suggests her growing awareness of the fact that her discourse rests on repetition rather than fact. When Hadria dismisses her arguments, Henriette can only reassert the primacy of her narrative: "You *won't* understand. I mean that motherhood has duties. You can't deny that" (340). When narratives are seen as fixed, denial and assent remain as the only options. As Henriette's use of imperatives such as "can't" and "won't," as well as her reliance on predetermined tales—such as duty and maternal affection— about motherhood, suggests, she views narratives in an either/or light: they will either prosper or become extinct, rather than being able to change and survive in a new form. As both the examples of Caird's non-fiction writing and Professor Fortescue suggest, authority cannot be achieved through repetition.

While Hadria's arguments question the monologic authority Henriette seeks refuge in, having to interact with this discourse forces Hadria to turn to her own body's experiences to understand her own actions. She realizes the need to have an "acquaintance" with motherhood "*per se.*" Responding to Henriette's recourse to empty narratives of "reason," "motherhood," and "duty," Hadria asserts:

> I am not discussing motherhood *per se*; no woman has yet been in a position to know what it is *per se*, strange as it may appear. No woman has yet experienced it apart from the enormous pressure of law and opinion that has, always, formed part of its inevitable conditions. The illegal mother is hounded by her fellows in one direction; the legal mother is urged and incited in another: free motherhood is unknown amongst us. I speak of it as it is. To speak of it *per se*, for the present, is to discuss the transcendental. (342)

This moment offers a new reading of her actions as a mother. In leaving her children, she is not enacting a new narrative with a fixed end point. Rather, she is making the current story of motherhood interactive, pushing at it from different "directions," refusing the "transcendental" and seeking the actual. She protests against motherhood "as it is," but more importantly her actions attempt to move toward a better understanding of motherhood "*per se,*" while admitting the indeterminacy of that narrative.

Most strikingly, Henriette's argument forces Hadria to acknowledge the material actuality of bodies acting in response to instinct. Early on in the text her brother protests that "there *are* such things as natural instincts," to which Hadria replies "there *are* such things as acquired tricks" (23). Caird paints instinct as one of the most pernicious narratives in the text, encapsulated by Hubert Temperley's confident assertion that evolutionary "philosophy" is merely a way to "throw[] off all the trammels...of duty and common sense" (77). In her discussion with Henriette, though, Hadria admits that instinct does play a role, arguing that motherhood "weaves cords of [woman's] own love and instinct" (341). In this moment the interaction between Hadria and Henriette's dialogues is clear, but so too is the indeterminacy of seemingly set narratives. Authority becomes a relative term; Henriette will not suddenly switch sides and, as Hadria implores her, begin to "use your ability on behalf of your sex instead of against it" so that "women would have cause to bless you, for all time" (339), but neither will her arguments sweep away Hadria's very real concerns. Breaking down the power of the unspoken, implicitly accepted discourse of motherhood, Hadria and Henriette each shift in how they approach the subject and what actual maternity entails. Only by returning to the experiences of her own body can Hadria shatter the authority motherhood has over all women's bodies throughout the entire text.

Hadria's addition of instinct to her own more radical narrative about motherhood allows us to return to and re-understand previous moments in the text. For Hadria actually takes a child with her to Paris, Martha, the illegitimate child of the village school-mistress (in a shocking plot twist, we later discover that Hadria's would-be lover is the father). When Hadria first adopts the child, the action seems "inconsistent," as another character terms it, because she "say[s] that children have been the means, from time immemorial, of enslaving women" but "go[es] and adopt[s] one of [the] enslavers!" (190). Analyzing the significance of this action in light of her declaration that motherhood should be understood *per se*, however, we can read Hadria's actions as a test of the parameters of the narrative around motherhood. The non-coerced mothering of an orphan is a very different form of motherhood than the legal maternity Hadria flees, and causes far less oppression while materially benefiting the survival and development of the child. In her declaration to Henriette, Hadria splits motherhood into two mutually exclusive categories: "illegal" and "hounded" or "legal" and "incited." By tracking how Hadria interacts with an actual, corporeal child, rather than battling with abstract authoritative pronouncements about motherhood, Caird suggests that the interactions of bodies offer far more possibilities than the discourse suggests.[14]

Instinct does serve a certain role here, but it is the instinct to seek out productive change rather than to replicate the status quo. With Martha, Hadria equates mothering with the encouragement of interaction and indeterminacy. When she adopts Martha, Hadria sees the child in explicitly experimental terms. "The little creature interests me," she says; "It is a tiny field for the exercise of the creative forces" (190). As Martha begins to grow, she surprises Hadria by being very responsive to changed conditions:

Her protectress had expected to have to do battle with hereditary weakness on account of her mother's sufferings, but the child shewed no signs of this. Either the common belief that mental trouble in the mother is reflected in the child was unfounded, or the evil could be overcome by the simple beneficence of pure air, good food, and warm clothing. (246)

Martha, a child of a "fallen woman," doomed, if one believes the plethora of Victorian narratives on the subject, to a life of shame, represents the clash of authority and body. Hadria explicitly states, using very evolutionary terms, that she wishes to equip Martha to succeed in the battle of life:

she has to make her way in the world. She must not be too meek... I want her... to be strengthened for the battle by a good long draught of happiness, and to be armed with that stoutest of all weapons--perfect health. (246)

In the opening pages of *The Origin*, Darwin writes that

any being, if it vary however slightly in any manner profitable to itself, under the complex and sometimes varying conditions of life, will have a better chance of surviving, and thus be naturally selected. From the strong principle of inheritance, any selected variety will tend to propagate its new and modified form. (5)

The propagation of fit offspring, Hadria's relations with Martha suggest, represents a form of motherly instinct based on interaction rather than just replication. Further, the ability to create change impels maternal instinct: once Martha begins to respond to her ministrations, Hadria "began to feel a more personal interest in her charge...She felt the relationship to be a true one, in contradistinction to the more usual form of protectorate of woman to child" (240).

The problem with Hadria's own children, whom she abandons in favor of Martha, lies in the fact that their existence seems to reify a set narrative, and thus bolster the authoritative take on maternity, rather than encourage open-endedness. Hadria muses that

throughout history...children had been the unfailing means of bringing women into line with tradition. Who could stand against them? They had been able to force the most rebellious to their knees. An appeal to the maternal instinct had quenched the hardiest spirit of revolt. No wonder the instinct had been so trumpeted and exalted! Women might harbour dreams and plan insurrections; but their children—little ambassadors of the established and expected—were argument enough to convince the most

hardened sceptics. Their helplessness was more powerful to suppress
revolt than regiments of armed soldiers. (87)

As "ambassadors of the established and expected," children enforce the
stability that narratives such as Henriette's require, rather than encouraging
interaction. Further, they represent a shutting down of alternate
possibilities, "suppress[ing]" the "dreams and plan[s]" of women,
exemplified in Hadria's attempt to become a musician. And they do so
through attacking the body: they "force" "quench" and "suppress." The
physical language of this moment stresses the interconnection between the
body and authoritative discourse, and Hadria's activities with Martha
demonstrate that change must be effected through actual bodies interacting.

While countless authorities used Darwinian thought to reinforce the
"instinctual" necessity of maternal self-sacrifice, evolutionary theory also
insists upon the primacy of the organism. *The Origin* declares that "natural
selection cannot possibly produce any modification in any one species
exclusively for the good of another species" (200). Caird suggests that the
mother, as well as the child, benefits from properly developed
motherhood. Not only is the mother gratified by the ability to develop and
strengthen the child, but the child encourages the mother to continue to
court variation. In Paris, Caird writes, "the child gave a sense of freshness
and youth to the little *ménage*. She made the anxieties easier to bear"
(328). In one of the most extended scenes featuring Martha and Hadria,
Martha is described as an "iconoclas[t]." Hadria builds houses of blocks
for her, which Martha then knocks down. While Hadria protests "I must
have my fairy palace; I won't have it pulled down," Martha inexorably
destroys it (329). Unlike Hadria, who at moments still yearns, like the
Professor, to counter one authority with a different, but still stable,
authority, Martha destroys the infrastructure of her world.[15] She physically
tears down the prior discourse, and creates the necessity for building a new
one rather than replacing it with a ready made authority. She also focuses
on action rather than reflection. The child offers a vision of another way of
living, based on variation rather than permanence. Caird suggests that the
adults of the world must temper this rashness with moderation, but still
hold to the directive for change. While Hadria's legitimate children, who
represent her acquiescence to authority serve as "ambassadors of the
expected," the adopted Martha offers a glimpse of the new configurations
that might be (literally) built, one block at a time.

Evolutionary biology explicitly provides this freedom to focus on
process and potential. "While presenting an ontology of life," Elizabeth
Grosz writes, "Darwin also provokes a concern with the possibilities of
becoming, and becoming-other, inherent in culture, which are also the

basic concerns of feminist and other political and social activists" (19-20). *Daughters* has frequently been read as a chronicle of the failure of evolutionary theory because every attempt to rewrite prescripted narratives through recourse to evolution fails miserably. I think it more useful to read it as a valorization of certain elements and techniques of evolutionary theory, those I have termed Darwinian dialogism. The great boon of evolution is its indeterminacy, its refusal to validate old narratives or to follow in previously trodden paths. Authority becomes a moot point in this free for all, and the experiences of bodies constantly shape and reshape the possible narratives.

Fiction is, as Bakhtin reminds us, the ultimate venue for competing narratives. For Caird this heteroglossic environment impels the interaction and reshaping of narratives. In contemplating her motives for adopting Martha, Hadria muses that "that poor woman's story touched me closely" (189). When she has to return from Paris because of her mother's illness, Hadria has a similar moment of narrative connection:

> She realized now, with agonising vividness, the sadness of her mother's life, the long stagnation, the slow decay of disused faculties, and the ache that accompanies all processes of decay, physical or moral. Not only the strong appeal of old affection, entwined with the earliest associations, was at work, but the appeal of womanhood itself: – the grey sad story of a woman's life, bare and dumb and pathetic. (362)

If, as Caird argues, women had been major factors in their own subjugation, promoting a cult of self-sacrifice and "pampering up their sickly virtue, at the expense of their sex" (471), women also hold the possibility of engendering change. Every time Hadria codifies experience as a "story" rather than "fate" or "duty," she makes it a text necessarily open to the interaction and indeterminacy of Darwinian dialogism. By 1894, there was nothing in the least revolutionary about Caird's claims that women deserved independence and basic rights. Instead, she differs by making her argument *evolutionary*, tracking the minute changes and variations in both narrative and body that might ultimately lead to female emancipation through the indeterminacy impelled by interaction.

Works Cited

Bakhtin, Mikhail. *The Dialogic Imagination: Four Essays*. Trans. C. Emerson and M, Holquist. Ed. M. Holquist. Austin, TX: University of Texas Press, 1990.

Beer, Gillian. *Darwin's Plots: Evolutionary Narrative in Darwin, George Eliot and Nineteenth-Century Fiction*. Second Ed. Cambridge, UK: Cambridge UP, 2000.

—. *Open Fields: Science in Cultural Encounter*. Oxford, England: Oxford UP, 1996.

Caird, Mona. *The Daughters of Danaus*. New York: The Feminist P, 1989.

—. "A Defence of the So-Called Wild Woman" *The Nineteenth Century* 31 (May 1892). 811-29.

—. "Marriage." *A New Woman Reader: Fiction, Articles, and Drama of the 1890s*. Ed. Carolyn Christensen Nelson. Ontario, Canada: Broadview P, 2001. 185-198.

—. "The Sanctuary of Mercy." 189?. *Victorian Women Writers Project*. Ed. Perry Willett. 2003. 24 March 2006. <http://www.indiana.edu/~letrs/vwwp/caird/sanctuary.html>

Darwin, Charles. *On the Origin of Species*. Cambridge, MA: Harvard UP, 2001.

Dilke, M.M. "The Appeal Against Female Suffrage: A Reply. II. *A New Woman Reader: Fiction, Articles, and Drama of the 1890s*. Ed. Carolyn Christensen Nelson. Ontario, Canada: Broadview P, 2001.. 131-5.

Fawcett, Millicent Garrett. "The Appeal Against Female Suffrage: A Reply. I" *A New Woman Reader: Fiction, Articles, and Drama of the 1890s*. Ed. Carolyn Christensen Nelson. Ontario, Canada: Broadview P, 2001. 124-130.

Foucault, Michel. *The History of Sexuality: An Introduction*. Volume I. Trans Robert Hurley. New York: Vintage Books, 1990.

Gates, Barbara T. *Kindred Nature: Victorian and Edwardian Women Embrace the Living World*. Chicago, Il: U of Chicago P, 1998.

Grand, Sarah. *The Heavenly Twins*. Cassell Publishing Company, 1893.

Grosz, Elizabeth. *The Nick of Time: Politics, Evolution and the Untimely*. New York: Crows Nest, NSW Allen & Unwin, 2004

Haraway, Donna J. *Simians, Cyborgs and Women: The Reinvention of Nature*. New York, NY: Routledge UP, 1991.

Harvey, H.E. "Science and the Rights of Women" *A New Woman Reader: Fiction, Articles, and Drama of the 1890s*. Ed. Carolyn Christensen Nelson. Ontario, Canada: Broadview P, 2001.. 168-9.

Ledger, Sally. *The New Woman: Fiction and Feminism at the Fin de Siécle*. New York, St Martin's P, 1997.

Levine, George. *Darwin and the Novelists: Patterns of Science in Victorian Fiction*. Cambridge: Harvard UP, 1988.

Pykett, Lynn. "The Cause of Women and the Course of Fiction: The Case of Mona Caird." *Gender Roles and Sexuality in Victorian Literature*. Ed. Christopher Parker. Brookfield, VT: Ashgate, 1995. 128-42.

Richardson, Angelique. *Love and Eugenics in the Late Nineteenth Century: Rational Reproduction and the New Woman*. Oxford: Oxford UP, 2003.

Stutfueld, Hugo. "Tommyrotics." *A New Woman Reader: Fiction, Articles, and Drama of the 1890s*. Ed. Carolyn Christensen Nelson. Ontario, Canada: Broadview P, 2001. 234-42.

Youngkin, Molly. *Feminist Realism at the* Fin de Siecle*: The Influence of the Late-Victorian Woman's Press on the Development of the Novel*. Columbus, OH: The Ohio State UP, 2007.

Notes

[1] In claiming that the New Woman, and Caird in particular, theoretically benefitted from Darwinian ideas, I am varying from a common critical discourse that tends to read such evolutionary moments in a Foucauldian sense. Sally Ledger, for instance, writes that "a major characteristic of Caird's novel is its negotiation of late nineteenth-century evolutionary discourses in an attempt to work out their implications for women. That these implications finally transpire to be almost wholly negative in their import…is perhaps indicative of the problems inherent of working within the hegemonical language of the dominant discourse… By contesting the logic of evolutionism in its own terms, Mona Caird's challenge in *The Daughters of Danaus* is from its inception radically limited" (27). If we see writers such as Caird as not echoing the language of Darwinism, but rather participating in shaping the discourse, we can begin to see the potential uses of Darwinian thinking to feminism. As Foucault himself writes, while "power is exercised from innumerable points," this power "from below" does not lead to monolithic power structures but rather "redistributions, realignments, homogenizations, serial arrangements, and convergences of the force relations" (94).

[2] While "evolutionary" may perhaps be a more accurate term in that I am not drawing a precise intellectual history—while Caird certainly read Darwin, she also read Huxley and Spencer and interacted with Karl Pearson and other members of the Men and Women's Club—I continue to use "Darwinian" for two interrelated

reasons. First, I argue that Caird was not simply embracing a hazy teleological vision of progress but rather was interested in the specific processes by which change was effected. Second, I want to stress that Caird (and other women writers who seriously engaged with evolutionary thought) operated within a scientific milieu as much as a cultural one—I do not want to draw a distinction between male scientists and female "dabblers."

[3] For a fully fleshed out discussion of the relationship between language and evolutionary theory, see Gillian Beer's *Open Fields*.

[4] Indeed, Bakhtin's definition of "dialogized heteroglossia" posits language as existing within a "concrete," almost material, "environment in which it lives and takes shape" (272). Language thus exists within a specific environment and shapes and is shaped by that environment: "the linguistic and stylistic profile of a given element (lexical, semantic, syntactic) is shaped by that subordinated unity to which it is most immediately proximate. At the same time this element, together with its most immediate unity, figures into the style of the whole, itself supports the accent of the whole and participates in the process whereby the unified meaning of the who is structured and revealed" (262).

[5] While her anti-vivisection texts, which I use to demonstrate her Darwinian dialogism, were not directly about evolutionary theory, the anti-vivisection movement drew much of its rhetorical fire from the kinship between all species (Frances Cobbe repeatedly urged Darwin to attach his name to the anti-vivisection petition sent up to Parliament). Barbara Gates traces the interconnection between evolutionary theory, women's political activity and anti-vivisection in *Kindred Spirits*, arguing that "in the latter decades of the nineteenth century, as women came more and more to redefine themselves politically and economically by seeking the vote and the right to work, they also became active in describing other species and in protecting animals in both their own and in foreign countries from threats like vivisection, hunting, and deforestation" (4).

[6] A number of Caird's contemporaries tended to rest upon the argument that evolution required women to advance socially rather than parsing out exactly how they saw the discourse of evolution as benefitting feminism. Ultimately both approaches failed: the latter because a far larger conservative base appropriated evolutionary discourse as a justification of female inferiority, while Caird's approach lacked the heady assurance and simplicity of her contemporaries's. However, I would argue that Caird's offers a viable model for a feminism allied with evolutionary science, both in terms of content and metaphorical force.

[7] Lyn Pykett argues that "Caird's nonfiction essays tend to present one voice on social issues whereas the fictional work tends to be more multi-vocal, allowing for disagreement on social issues between characters" (140). My reading suggests otherwise, but significantly, I focus on Caird's work about vivisection, a scientific topic, rather than Pykett, who focuses on her feminist writings. Thus I would venture to argue that the scientific topic of the anti-vivisection work encourages the interaction and polyvocality Caird also embraced in her fiction.

---

[8] "After Darwin," writes George Levine, "the ideal of disinterested observation came under increasing pressure" (65). Levine argues that post-Darwin, the observer was always, in a sense, observing him or herself and in danger of becoming object rather than subject. At the same time, "observation…implied an alternative to traditional authority, to the dominance of ancient institutions, but particularly to the dominance of the word, of texts" (211).

[9] Gillian Beer argues that Darwin himself was very aware of the way that he was evolving narratives for new purposes: Darwin "sought to appropriate and to recast inherited mythologies, discourses, and narrative orders. He was telling a new story, against the grain of the language available to tell it in" (*Darwin's Plots* 3).

[10] The professor is, of course, also problematic in that he is male. It's hard not to read the investment of the masculine body with scientific and moral authority as an ideological failure of sorts: does Caird merely ape "'ologies and 'isms" handed down from wiser sources? As Fortescue's failure as a redeemer demonstrates, Caird does not depend on masculine science to save the day.

[11] Recent feminist theorists of science stress biology's powerful narrative pull. "Surely scientific stories are not innocent," writes Donna Harway; "no class of tales can be free of rules for narrating a proper story within a particular genre" (106).

[12] Recall that even in triumphant polemics such as that at the end of "Marriage," Caird emphasizes that the power of evolution is in its potentiality, based on the human observer interacting with varying condition: "we are no longer entirely blind," she points out; "we see a limitless field of endless possibility" (198).

[13] It is worth noting that the majority of New Woman writers tended to valorize maternal instinct. Many New Women turned to Darwinian terminology to bolster their political aims, relying on the figure of woman as mother of the species to support the claims for greater female rights. For instance, in *The Heavenly Twins* Grand paints the New Woman as better than the best old mother: "whatever defects in character the new women may eventually acquire, lack of maternal affection will not be one of them" (288). Angelique Richardson suggests that a "maternalist agenda" surfaced among New Women as a "eugenic feminism" that constructed a "civic motherhood which sought political recognition for reproductive labor" (9).

[14] Hadria actually has two sons with Temperley, but they are almost invisible in the text: indeed, we only learn about them through a reported conversation of a village person reporting what she has heard about them. I would suggest the fact that they are indeed boys, and proper heirs, with all the repulsive associations that represents to Hadria, makes them less viable options for mothering than female, illegitimate Martha. Most distressing to Hadria, however, I would argue, is the fixity of their positions. In her discussion with Henriette she terms her position vis-à-vis the children she has had with Hubert as that of "an intelligent and trustworthy superintendent, whose services assured the children's welfare" (340). As a

superintendent, Hadria carries out desires rather than enacts her own—she "assures" rather than decides.

[15] Perhaps Martha's own illegitimacy serves as a tool to furnish her anti-establishment actions.

CHAPTER FOUR

MONA CAIRD AND THE SPECTACLE
OF SUFFERING

CASEY A. COTHRAN

In her afterward to the 1989 Feminist Press publication of *The Daughters of Danaus*, Margaret Morganroth Guellette celebrates the fact that Mona Caird's deeply depressed main character does not commit suicide at the end of the novel, thus separating herself from many other proto-feminist heroines. Guellette writes, "The temptation to martyr Hadria must have been great. Caird was deeply, consciously, interested in writing feminist tragedy. She believed that the *normal* life of women was potentially tragic – painful, wrenching, unnatural, and full of suffering" (509). Guellette continues,

> In relishing Caird's brave decision to let Hadria live, we should recall the powerful influence of the European fictional tradition that kills women [...]. The existence of *The Daughters of Danaus* forces us to rethink that tradition, meaning not only such works as Rousseau's *Julie* (1761), Goethe's *Elective Affinities*(1812), Flaubert's *Madame Bovary* (1857), and Tolstoy's *Anna Karenina* (1877), but also Eliot's *Mill on the Floss* (1860), Schreiner's *Story of an African Farm* (1883), and some later feminist novels in which women die. (513)

As she completes her discussion of the novel, Guellette isolates what she sees as one of the key strengths of the piece: "we can use *The Daughters of Danaus* to tell another story, of a countertradition that privileges not martyrdom but endurance" (518).

Caird's choice to keep her suffering heroine alive is indeed a notable and noteworthy one. It is interesting, however, to investigate the descriptions of physical and mental pain that do permeate this novel, if a primary narrative that describes the heroine's eventual death does not. Here I will argue that the vision of "endurance" that Caird sets forth in *The Daughters of Danaus* serves as a striking exploration of the ways in which suffering can convey meaning. In this text, physical infirmity is linked to social oppression. The heroine recognizes that the weakening of her physical body is a direct result of acting as daughter, housewife, and mother. Nevertheless, Hadria's open acknowledgement of her misery (and its domestic cause) allows her to warn others of the corrosive nature of traditional women's roles. It will be my argument that Hadria's character explores how a woman might visibly dramatize her suffering in order to bring to fruition new paths for other women. By making her own painful confinement within the domestic sphere into a sad spectacle, Hadria encourages others to re-envision the roles of all women in late Victorian culture.

Additionally, I would argue that Caird's novel can be seen as part of a larger cultural examination of the violence enacted on women's bodies in the decades both preceding and following the turn of the century. It acts as a marker between the 1888-1891 murders of Jack the Ripper (where a man was believed to have gruesomely destroyed women's bodies) and the militant feminist suffragettes of the early twentieth century (who did violence on their own bodies for political gain). As noted by Judith R. Walkowitz in *City of Dreadful Delight: Narratives of Sexual Danger in Late-Victorian London*, the Ripper murders became "part of a formative moment in the production of feminist sexual politics" (2). It will be my argument that Caird's *The Daughters of Danaus*, published in 1894, three years after the last murder, evidences new ways of interpreting the damaged bodies of women, positing suffering not as a sign of victimization but as a means of protest. Furthermore, just as Hadria's open acknowledgement of her illness turns domestic roles into subjects for investigation and critique, real women living in the decades after the novel's publication harmed themselves in an effort to demand interpretive control, to make women's inequality in society a tangible object of horror. The "militant movement" of 1900-1914 featured suffragettes who risked both assault and jail time, who participated in dramatic hunger strikes, all in their efforts to win for women the right to vote.

It is not my argument that these three cultural stories of women's suffering are directly related, but it does seem that looking at them together allows the modern scholar to trace a shifting pattern of cultural perspectives on women and suffering. It is assumed that Caird's fictional work reacted to and interacted with a national audience, participating in a critical discourse about women's bodies within that society. As written art both reflects and constructs public concepts of individual subjectivity, this study recognizes how literature reproduces national assumptions, fears, and dreams at the same time that it positions the readers of this literature as consumers of a particular writer's ideological bent. Even though the modern scholar can not directly link Caird's novel with the Whitechapel murders or with the specific acts of suffragettes, it does appear that *The Daughters of Danaus* illustrates an important shift in the way women viewed the female body, and specifically its potential to act symbolically and authoritatively. Somewhere between 1888 and 1914, some feminists took up the idea that social empowerment can arise from vocal, dramatic disregard for personal health.

The authors, artists, public figures, and ordinary people involved in the New Woman Movement of the 1890s attempted to redefine, deconstruct, or critique the ideological formulation of woman and of woman's social and biological destiny. In her discussion of the "popular appeal" of feminism at the end of the nineteenth century, Ann Heilmann notes that "The enthusiasm with which feminist ideas were taken up by young middle-class women and modified into claims for personal liberty and equality of opportunity testifies to the success of the social project on which New Woman writers were engaged" (9, 5). Certainly the efforts of these women to promote ideas of change, "to disrupt taken-for-granted assumptions and dogmatic complacencies," enabled individuals to critique – and to change – the legal and social conditions that resulted in the oppression of women (Felski 14). The Married Woman's Property Act of 1882, the Infants Bill of 1886, and the Separation and Maintenance Act of 1895 all granted women political rights in regards to property ownership and child custody.[1] In the next quarter century, women would entrench themselves in the workforce and achieve the right to vote.

What seems to have brought about these changes is in part the examination of lived women's experience that can be found in New Woman novels. These examinations, although intended to reveal the ideologies that defined and delimited the female sex, often were constructed as representations of "real" life. Many authors struggled to articulate activist discourses by exploring the tragic experiences of female characters in the setting of the modern world. And indeed, issues of freedom and constraint appear to have haunted the lives of feminist activists just as they haunted the texts of the New Woman genre. Ruth Brandon concludes her text on activist women living at the turn of the nineteenth century with the following statement:

> it is remarkable how few of these brilliant, forceful, ambitious women – and nearly all of them were that – managed to avoid living their lives on the terms of a male lover or husband. Eleanor Marx, Edith Ellis, Amber Reeves, even such obviously successful women as Beatrice Webb and

> Rebecca West – none of them managed to live their lives as they would
> have done had they been entirely free agents. And if it is argued that none
> of us are free agents, then one need only compare their lives with those of
> the men they were involved with. (249)

For the most part, the women's experiences described in New Woman novels are ones of frustrating limitations, if not of overt tragedy. As novelists of the mid- and late nineteenth-century illustrated the dehumanizing effect that intense industry had on members (often male) of the public labor force, prominent women such as Florence Nightingale, Harriet Martineau, and Caird herself described the ways in which domestic pursuits demoralized (real and fictional) women of ambition and purpose.

Despite their focus on the stifling quality of women's lives, a number of New Woman authors struggled (or failed) to imagine "New Ways" of living. This is not surprising; female characters who rejected normative womanly behavior asserted an identity whose nature and value were ambiguous at best and which had no defined space within traditional social structures. In *The Daughters of Danaus*, Hadria, Caird's heroine, is ultimately determined to embrace confinement and self-destruction. Poised precariously between positions of submission and self-assertion for the major parts of the text, her choice to accept her place in a claustrophobic domestic sphere often appears inevitable.

It is true that characters in *The Daughters of Danaus* imagine drastic rebellions, Hadria's sister Algitha embracing the practical details of mutinous action more successfully than her sister. Yet, despite the fact that the forces within culture are shown to unfairly – if not cruelly – constrain women, Caird claims that many women must reside in culture and thus acknowledge the limited potential of their lived reality. It is to be expected that the institutions of marriage and family will regulate and restrict the fates of women, particularly the fates of "presumptuous girls" in possession of sensitivity, talent, and intelligence. The title *The Daughters of Danaus* refers to the Greek myth that relates how forty-nine of the fifty daughters of Danaus, after being married *en masse*, murder their husbands on their wedding night in an effort to free themselves. As punishment for this crime, all forty-nine women are destined to draw water in sieves from bottomless wells – for eternity.[2] In keeping with the themes evoked by the text's title, Hadria, after her attempt to abandon her husband and children in order to become a composer in Paris, is destined to live out a life of tedious domestic activity: a fate comparable to the daughters' endless, useless drawing of water. Highlighting the historical tradition illustrated by the myth, Caird claims that the majority of rebellious women are doomed to such futile existences; near the end of the novel, Hadria announces, "See how feeble after all, are these pretentious women of the new order, who begin by denying the sufficiency of the life assigned them, by common consent, and end by failing in that and in the other which they aspire to" (471). By arguing that most women who try to escape the system become "ghastly failure[s]" that others may "point to" as reasons why women should not try to assert their independence in the first place (471), Caird claims that the system must be destroyed in other ways. If it cannot be escaped (and if the failure to escape ultimately "will add to the staggering weight that we all stumble under" [470], thus "hindering" further future young women of "talent" and "resolve" [470, 471]), it must be endured. Yet it is my argument that Caird does not give up on the dreams of "the women of the new order"; if women's roles are to be endured, they can be endured in such a way as to protest them.

In its examination of the lives of New Women, *The Daughters of Danaus* explores both the concept of escape and the concept of endurance. The novel begins with a midnight philosophical debate between Hadria and her three siblings: Fred, Ernest, and Algitha. The principal dispute exists between Ernest, who champions Emerson's claim "that circumstance can always be conquered" and Hadria, who argues that if Emerson had been "a girl," he would have known that "conditions *do* count hideously in one's life" (*Daughters* 10, 14). Hadria's sister frowns at this negative attitude and claims that women have the right to renounce unjust social "conditions," despite the social consequences that are sure to follow individual bouts of rebellious action. She claims, "If one is unjustly restrained…it is perfectly right to brave the infliction of the sort of pain that people feel only because they unfairly object to one's liberty of action" (15). Nevertheless, Hadria responds to this passionate assertion with a reference to the practical circumstances that would result in such an "infliction"; she argues

> But what a frightful piece of circumstance *that* is to encounter…to have to buy the mere right to one's liberty by cutting through prejudices that are twined in with the very heart-strings of those one loves! Ah! *that* particular obstacle has held many a woman helpless and suffering, like some wretched insect pinned alive to a board throughout a miserable lifetime! What would Emerson say to these cases? That "Nature magically suits the man to his fortunes by making these the fruit of his character"? Pooh! I think Nature more often makes a man's fortunes a veritable shirt of Nessus which burns and clings, and finally kills him with anguish! (15)

Thus Caird introduces the idea that not all women will choose to escape the web of familial and social forces that keep them in the domestic sphere. Though they may be miserable in the lives they are pressured to lead, moral or emotional integrity (and not weakness) can drive them to give up on dreams of self-actualization. This passage in particular foreshadows Hadria's respect for the "heart-strings" of her loved ones; it is specifically the dread of destroying her mother's health that will cause Hadria to take up a traditional domestic life. Mrs. Fullerton, dangerously ill after her two daughters' rejection of domestic responsibilities, says, "Tell Hadria to come home if she does not want to kill me" (364). Without hesitation, Hadria comes home.

Notably, the imagery in the above passage foreshadows the nature of Hadria's future suffering, just as its content foreshadows the novel's plot. In this segment of text and elsewhere, disturbing images of bodily suffering are used to depict the (often unseen) ravages of emotional anguish. Here Hadria calls forth the evocative image of an insect "pinned alive to a board"; her reference to the shirt of Nessus also brings to mind the grisly spectacle of Hercules committing suicide as he throws himself onto a funeral pyre.[3] Like Hercules, who destroys himself in order to avoid the pain caused by an invisible poison, Hadria can be seen as a figure whose bodily decay serves as a symptom of the more painful mental and emotional suffering she experiences.

Similar explorations of the devastating potential of family to manipulate women appear throughout Caird's fictional writings. In her earlier novel, *The Wing of Azrael*, the heroine, Viola, tells her father that she has no wish to marry, that she would like the opportunity to make a living for herself. His response is furiously derisive:

> Do you know what a woman is who does not marry? I will tell you: she is a cumberer of the ground, a devourer of others' substance, a failure, a wheel that won't turn; she has no meaning; she is in the way; she ought never to have been born. She is neglected, despised, left out; and who cares whether she lives or dies? She is alone, scorned and derided, without office, without object, without the right to exist. (*Azrael* 80)

Viola is the youngest and only daughter in a family of boys, and pressure is placed on her to restore the squandered family fortune by marrying Philip, her wealthy (and depraved) neighbor. Through her father, Caird's heroine is reminded "not only that the sole career open to her was marriage" but that "she must make deliberate efforts to secure it for herself, or to aid and abet in schemes which others undertook on her behalf. She must bestir herself in the matter, for it was her appointed business" (*Azrael* 80). It is after her father's fierce attack on her ideas that Caird describes Viola's experiencing a "strange desperate pleasure in self-torture" (*Azrael* 81). After her mother points out to her that her "father, her brothers, all are depending on her decision" to marry so that they might keep their family home, Viola miserably submits to Philip's proposal (*Azrael* 129).

Like Viola, Hadria dwells repeatedly on the feelings of mental and physical pain that she experiences as a result of capitulating to the wishes of her family. As she sits by her mother's sickbed, Hadria has a moment of insight, hearing the demands not only of her mother, but "of womanhood itself: – the grey sad story of a woman's life, bare and dumb and pathetic in its irony and pain: the injury from without, and then the self-injury, its direct offspring; unnecessary, yet inevitable" (*Daughters* 362-63). In this passage, Caird writes that "injury from without" leads directly to "self-injury". This description is striking; it indicates that suppressed women will eventually take charge of their own pain. Although this may seem a disturbing claim, it is, in its own way, a form of empowerment. In both *The Wing of Azrael* and *The Daughters of Danaus*, individual women are seen as *choosing* to harm themselves. Both Hadria and Viola participate in their own oppression, and thus they form conscious responses to the restrictions of an unjust society. Specifically, in *The Daughters of Danaus*, Hadria herself determines to make amends for causing her mother to fall ill. Caird writes, "Hadria's whole thought and strength were now centered on the effort to bring about [...] propitiation, in her own person. She prepared the altar and sharpened the knife" (363). Again, Caird uses dramatic physical imagery to describe the emotional pain her heroine is prepared to undergo. She also writes in such a way as to place her heroine in charge of her own pain.

Yet, in addition to embracing a life of suffering, Caird argues that Hadria needs to express the futility and tragedy of this life to others. As the novel begins, Hadria seems resigned to the limited life she is destined, as a woman, to lead; looking out over the snow-covered fields outside her home, she exclaims, "Life is as white and as unsympathetic as this.... We just dance our reel in our garret, and then it is all over; and whether we do the steps as our fancy would have them, or a little otherwise [...] – heavens and earth, what does it matter?" (*Daughters* 13). Certainly this particular quotation seems to indicate a cynical resignation to a pre-determined life of impotence and ineffectuality. However, Caird as author possesses strong feelings on women's inability to "do the steps as [their] fancy would have them." This is made evident both in Caird's widely read non-fiction writings on marriage, history, and human development and in her continuing descriptions of her fictional character's fierce frustration with her limited opportunities for personal and artistic expression. Although she takes a flippant tone early in the novel, eventually Hadria will learn to rage against her life circumstances. Later in the text, Caird presents one of Hadria's letters to her sister, Algitha:

> The more I see of life, the more hideous seems the position that women hold in relation to the social structure, and the more sickening the current nonsense that is talked about us and our "missions" and "spheres." It is so feeble, so futile, to try to ornament an essentially degrading fact. It is such insolence to talk to us – good heavens, to *us!* – about holiness and sacredness, when men (to whom surely a sense of humor has been denied) divide their women into two great classes, both of whom they insult and enslave, insisting peremptorily on the existence of each division, but treating one class as private and the other as public property. One might as well talk to driven cattle in the shambles about their "sacred mission" as to women. It is an added mockery, a gratuitous piece of insolence. (306-07)

Such vociferous condemnation of the "two great classes of women" is key to this text. It is only after she has explored every alternative identity available to her that Hadria truly embraces a life of meaningful suffering. At first, in response to her misery, Hadria will consider having an adulterous affair. Ultimately however, after hearing of the local schoolmistress who has died after being seduced, impregnated, and abandoned, she concludes that neither the celebrated nor the fallen woman is able to achieve a life that is not somehow degrading. Because the position of the adulteress is just as perilous as that of wife, Hadria will decide to maintain her status as wife to Hubert Temperly. This position is one she has worked to renounce and reject; however, when faced with an effective means of doing so – through the sexual betrayal of her husband and the physical renunciation of her marriage vows – she is unable to act. The consequence would place her in a sphere which she dreads just as strongly as the domestic.

In addition to exploring the potentials of domestic and of fallen womanhood, Caird briefly considers her heroine's potential to escape this limiting social dichotomy. Midway through the text, in a radical move, Hadria decides to leave her unhappy life, as well as her husband and children. Abandoning family and friends, she escapes from England in order to begin a musical career in Paris. For a time, she experiences the joys of an independent, artistic life. However, this attempt at escape is neither permanent nor successful. The brevity of this section of the novel is striking, as is Hadria's continuing frustration with her lack of time in which to work. Hadria delights in the fact that she is finally free to compose and study her music; however, as Patricia Murphy notes, "*The Daughters of Danaus* responds to the same concerns articulated by Victorian women writers who decried the incessant claims of domestic and social routine upon their time, thereby limiting or precluding the pursuit of other interests" (154). Hadria must continue to make calls on friends, to write little letters, and to look after her adopted daughter Martha. Even though she may live independently, the household tasks that characterize a woman's life are shown to be inescapable. In turn, the narrator explains that Hadria is hindered by her immense artistic talent. Hadria cannot make a living by selling her compositions, as they are too original. Caird writes, "only very slowly would the quality of the music be recognized by even the more cultivated public. [...] It was rebel music, offensive to the orthodox" (321).

Within *The Daughters of Danaus*, the character of Valeria duPrel makes a living writing novels about radical, successful, independent women. Nevertheless, Caird herself seems determined not to write about such women but rather about modern daughters of Danaus. Because her heroine escapes only for a short while, and because her drastic behavior calls forth serious consequences, the reader is left to conclude that Caird wishes to focus on women fighting injustice within the social system rather than women who attack it from without. And so begins Caird's exploration of meaningful, expressive suffering. The cause of suffering is clear: besieged first by her family's demands on her time and then by the myriad needs of her husband and children, Hadria experiences thwarted musical genius and limited energy. In *The Daughters of Danaus*, the heroine is not faced with a violent and vindictive spouse (such as Viola Sedley faces in *The Wing of Azrael*), but rather with an ordinary and dull one. This itself is a radical move, as Caird argues that it is not merely a bad husband – but any husband – who may destroy and depress a woman of vivacity, intelligence, and potential.

Indeed, Caird argues that marriage is an instigator of both physical and mental decay. Specifically, as Hadria considers her married state, she decides that

> She felt twenty years older since her marriage. She wondered why it was that marriage did not make all women wicked, – openly and actively so. If ever there was an arrangement by which every evil instinct and every spark of the devil was likely to be aroused and infuriated, surely the customs and traditions that clustered round this estate constituted that dangerous condition! Hardship, difficulty, tragedy could be faced, but not the humiliating, the degrading, the contemptible.... Most women, she found, ranked certain elements very differently, with lavish use of halos and gilding in their honor, feeling perhaps, she hinted, the dire need of such external decoration. (168)

There is a definite physical aspect to Hadria's mental distress; here, she feels "twenty years older since her marriage." Later, a friend notes, "Hadria shewed signs of serious trouble. The haggard lines, the marks of suffering, were not to be hidden" (420). Ultimately, it seems that Caird refers to the physical consequences of unhappiness in order to reshape the ways in which the material conditions of the body and the figurative "conditions" of women's lives might be understood. By translating abstract emotional pain into quantifiable descriptions of physical weakness, the author emphasizes the corrosive nature of the relationship between the individual body and the social body. Women like Hadria serve as signifiers of cultural distress, and indeed, as the above passage asserts, the "dangerous condition" of being a married woman in bourgeois society poses a threat to the health of "all women". Here, Caird appears to be claiming that the weakness (and nervous hysteria) often associated with the female sex actually serve as indicators of the corruption of "the customs and traditions" delimiting women's public and private roles within their culture. Caird also indicates in the above passage that, unlike Hadria, many women seem unaware of these issues, though they do possess a powerful "need" to see themselves as angelic, their social positions as somehow worthy of special honor. Hadria observes that, for many women, a life of degradation can be endured if it is linked with a sense of superiority.

In *The Daughters of Danaus*, Caird destabilizes traditional narratives of female suffering. Her heroine chooses to comply with the forces that urge her to take on distressing and restrictive social roles, but she also chooses not to be happy. She refuses to describe womanly self-sacrifice as worthy of "halos and gilding," but rather denounces it as "degrading" and "contemptible" (168). She tells her emancipated sister,

> "The one thing I won't do, is to be virtuously resigned. And I won't 'make the best of it.' […] If my life is to bear testimony to the truth, its refrain ought to be, 'This is wrong, this is futile, this is cruel, this is damnable.' I shall warn every young woman I come across, to beware." (473)

Caird has Hadria end her tirade:

> "It is for us to warn. I *won't* pretend to think that things are all right, when I know that they are not all right. That would be mean. What is called making the best of it, would testify all the wrong way. My life, instead of being a warning, would be a sort of trap. Let me at least play the humble role of scarecrow. I am in excellent condition for it," she added, grasping her thin wrist. (474)

The scarecrow is a significant symbol, often seen to represent a false or frightening imitation of life. Nevertheless, despite the fact that the body of the scarecrow is lifeless, this body possesses authority, warning off predators, guarding plants that provide sustenance for bodies that *are* real and functioning. Scarecrows are often given a prominent place, elevated, with arms outstretched. As Hadria embraces this identity, she simultaneously recognizes the lifeless existence she has accepted and the dynamic warning her wasted body might give to others. By speaking out about the unhappiness that marks her body as well as her psyche, Hadria will make others aware of her situation and thus protest it. Indeed, this form of protest is shown as a meaningful alternative for women who find themselves unable to escape the domestic sphere.

A familiar figure in England and Europe, scarecrows have been, for centuries, common parts of rural landscapes.[4] Some historians trace the origins of the scarecrow to farmers in Greece who would place carved wooden statues, often painted purple, of Priapus (the son of Dionysus and Aphrodite) in their fields. Priapus was said to possess an "ugly face and twisted body," and it was believed that his unsightly appearance inspired birds to keep away from grapes and wheat (Giblin and Ferguson 7). In *The Daughters of Danaus*, the scarecrow can be read using a number of strategies; on the most basic level, however, it seems to represent a "straw man" – a being who exists in a pathetic imitation of life. Like Priapus, the body of the scarecrow is described as disfigured in some way: in Hadria's case, her body is acknowledged to be malnourished and insubstantial. (Hadria grasps her "thin wrist", claiming she is in "excellent condition" for the part.) Hadria also recognizes the power of the scarecrow, celebrating its ability both to caution and to curse. Specifically, the scarecrow possesses the ability to "testify" – to speak to other young women, to warn them to "beware" at the same time that it serves as a visual reminder of "the truth" about domestic life.

It has been noted that, in the nineteenth century, self-denial could be viewed as a source of pride or as a form of power, even as an individual suffered from unhappiness because of it. John R. Reed, in his discussion of the Victorians' beliefs in moral and evolutionary progress, argues that

> Man's progress is related to his strength of will […], yet this strength of will takes the primary form of self-suppression in favor of a larger community or an ideal (political, social, or religious). Character becomes a denial of self, free will the suppression of the individual will. (90)

In the *Daughters of Danaus*, Caird both uses and critiques this concept. Hadria is socially encouraged to suppress her dreams of becoming a musician for the good of her husband, her children, and her mother. However, as the novel progresses, it appears that her choice to suppress her desires is not specifically based on her need to serve any of these individuals but rather as a means of protest. Her self-denial does exist to benefit "a larger community," but she re-envisions that community as a community of women, disregarding the family unit as an appropriate inspiration for woman's actions of self-sacrifice. (Indeed, capitulation to the demands of family becomes an object of critique.) Like the Victorians discussed above, Hadria's "self-suppression" is associated with both "character" and "progress". By bravely sacrificing her happiness (and thus her health), Hadria gains a tool she can use against the social strictures that have oppressed women for centuries.

In his work on masochism and the individual, Roy F. Baumeister postulates that "Masochism does not only take the self apart but also, to some extent, puts together a new set of meanings in place of the deconstructed one. The construction of new meanings may hold the major appeal for some masochists, whereas for others the removal of meaning is the primary attraction" (x). In *The Daughters of Danaus*, Hadria willingly acknowledges her self-destructive behavior in order to deconstruct the identity of "victim" and to replace that persona with a conceptualization of an actively, vocally tragic heroine.

There are a number of passages in the text that indicate Hadria's awareness that suffering can serve as a form of mutiny. Perhaps the most evocative is Hadria's discussion of a tree that has been unable to grow. She recalls, as a girl, being struck by the sight of

> "a young ash-tree that had got jammed into a chink so that it couldn't grow straight, or spread, as its inner soul, poor stripling, evidently inspired it to grow. Outside, there were hundreds of upright, vigorous, healthful young trees, fulfilling that innate idea in apparent gladness, and with obvious general advantage, since they were growing into sound, valuable trees, straight of trunk, nobly developed. I felt like the poor sapling in the cranny, that had just the same natural impetus of healthy growth as all the others, but was forced to become twisted, and crooked, and stunted and wretched. I think most women have to grow in a cranny. It is generally known as their Sphere. [...] I noticed [...] that the desperate struggle to grow of that young tree had begun to loosen the masonry of the edifice that cramped it. There was a great dangerous-looking crack right across the building. The tree was not saved from deformity, *but* it had its revenge! Some day that noble institution would come down by the run." (271-72)

The tree has become "twisted" and "deformed"; nevertheless, its "struggle" has resulted in a significant crack in the man-made structure that stunts its growth. It is notable that Caird has her heroine directly compare the plight of the tree with the life of her heroine; it is also notable that here Hadria uses the word "revenge" to describe the actions of the tree on the edifice. Revenge indicates a powerful action, a destructive force. The tree is no longer a casualty but an agent of change.

Through this passage and others, Caird indicates to readers that Hadria does have the power to make cracks in patriarchal strictures, despite her oppression. This power becomes available to her as she exposes unpleasant truths. As Hadria discusses the "disease" of "the present age" (255-56) with her friend Lady Engleton, she remarks that the modern world seems to her "[l]ike a creature beginning to struggle through a bad illness" (256). Hadria can illustrate these troubling social illnesses to others (and thus protest them) by exposing her own illness. Using terms that recall the dress and the composition of female bodies, she analyzes the society in which she lives, noting: "[I]t is pathetic, the way we have tried to make things decorative; but it won't hold out much longer. Women are driving their masters to plain speaking – the ornaments are being dragged down. [...] we venture to hint that this unsatisfactory skeleton may be modified in form" (257). By exposing both literal and figurative skeletons – the emaciated bodies of women and the ugly underpinnings that delineate women's social roles – women may protest the conditions of their lives.

Indeed, according to Caird, it appears that things must be made unpleasant: ornaments must be "dragged down" if women want "plain speaking." Although Hadria cannot be specifically labeled a "masochist," as she does not appear to enjoy the suffering she endures, criticism on masochists and their behaviors can help the modern scholar to understand some of the logic behind this heroine's actions. Gilles Deleuze writes, "The masochist's apparent obedience conceals a criticism and a provocation" (88). By submitting "with a vengeance" (Noble 5), the victim draws attention to the iniquitous behaviors of the oppressor. Certainly this seems a resourceful tactic for women who were destined to live within the ideological constraints of a particular time and culture. Marianne Noble, in her work on masochism and American sentimental literature writes, "Histrionic victimization is a particularly effective strategy for self-empowerment in a liberal society in which most citizens want to be seen as nonviolent and compassionate" (9). While her community views her escape to Paris with shock and disapproval, Hadria's gradual decay inspires her friends at least to talk and wonder about the things which have made her so sad and ill. Near the end of the novel Hadria herself concludes, "The great mass of [...] life showed itself as prose, because the significance of things had not been grasped or suspected; but here and there, the veil was pierced – by some suffering soul, by some poet's vision – and the darkness of our daily, pompous, careworn, ridiculous little existence made painfully visible" (479). The "suffering soul" (and, one imagines, the correspondent damaged body) is the one able to expose the ugly truths about life.

As Susan Wendell has observed, "People who do not appear or act physically 'normal' draw attention to the disciplines of normality. [...] there are rules at work, but most of us are trying to ignore the existence of the rules, trying to pretend that things are 'naturally' and effortlessly the way they seem, not socially enforced" (89). As Hadria becomes thinner and thinner, and as she remains unhappy, refusing to "make the best" of her circumstances, she draws emphasis to her crippled genius and to the social system that has harmed her. Caird writes, "it was impossible not to suffer. [...] Should someone gain by it, that was highly satisfactory, and more than could be said of most suffering, which exists, it would seem, only to increase and multiply after the manner of some dire disease. This was what Hadria dreaded in her own case: that the loss would not end with her" (370). Caird's heroine desires her suffering to be seen, and to have meaning. She wishes others, particularly future women, to "gain" by it.

Near the end of the novel, Caird describes her heroine as both deeply depressed and physically ill. Tormented from a state of enfeeblement, Hadria is affected by the dark, cold winter that haunts the countryside:

> The winter came suddenly. Some terrific gales had robbed the trees of their lingering yellow leaves, and the bare branches already shewed their exquisite tracery against the sky. Heavy rain followed, and the river was swollen, and there were floods that made the whole country damp, and rank, and terribly depressing. Mrs. Fullerton felt the influence of the weather, and complained of neuralgia and other ailments. She needed watching very carefully, and plenty of cheerful companionship. This was hard to supply. [...] Hadria feared, at times, that she would break down disastrously. She was frightened at the strange haunting ideas that came to her, the dread and nameless horror that began to prey upon her, try as she would to protect herself from these nerve-torments, which she could trace so clearly to their causes. If only, instead of making one half insane and stupid, the strain of grief would but kill one outright, and be done with it! (468-69)

As insidious and uncontrollable as the seasons, the normalizing machinations of civilization and the simplistic rounds of daily life have reduced "Mrs. Fullerton" to bare bones. One assumes after reading the passage that Caird envisions a whole country of weak women who suffer from exposure to an environment that is "damp, and rank, and terribly depressing."

Indeed, at least in her dreams, Hadria is not alone. Near the end of *The Daughters of Danaus*, she

> recalled a strange and grotesque vision, or waking-dream, that she had dreamt a few nights before: of a vast abyss, black and silent, which had to be filled up to the top with the bodies of women, hurled down to the depths of the pit of darkness, in order that the survivors might, at last, walk over in safety. Human bodies take but little room, and the abyss seemed to swallow them, as some greedy animal its prey. But Hadria knew, in her dream, that some day it would have claimed its last victim, and the surface would be level and solid, so that people would come and go, scarcely remembering that beneath their feet was once a chasm into which throbbing lives had to descend, to darkness and a living death. (451)

Significantly, Hadria imagines that it is not the *works* of living women that are needed to create a new world for the women of the future. Instead, their *bodies* are called forth to serve. These living forms are necessary to fill the pit. Despite her immense intellectual and artistic potential, in Caird's novel the New Woman imagines offering not these but her suffering body to the creation of a new world. It is the body that will have the most noticeable effect on "the abyss" of ignorance and despair which threatens to swallow women up; it is the accumulation of material, suffering bodies that will permit the woman of the future to move towards education, freedom, authority, and enlightenment. Thus, the theme of physical suffering takes on a centrality to the novel's moral structure. Sensory and corporal experience – both the gradual deterioration of Hadria's body and the violent destruction of the bodies in her dream – are equated with the necessary conditions for change.

In some sense, Hadria's vision is merely a "waking dream"; a more hopeful tone is taken following this passage as Hadria, Valeria duPrel, and Hadria's sister Algitha (who has become a successful philanthropic worker in London's East End) imagine the possibilities inherent in a future in which women have joined together to change the circumstances of their lives. As Sally Ledger notes, "Although a late twentieth-century feminist reading of Caird's novel might wish for a less deterministic narrative, the close of the novel is more open-ended than the general drift of the narrative might have led a reader to expect. And history, arguably, has vindicated both its dominant gradualist vision and its proposal for a feminist 'sisterhood' against oppression" (30). However, despite the vision of sisterhood and hope that ends the narrative, much of that hope is built on the knowledge of present suffering. In Hadria's mind (and perhaps in Caird's mind, as well), the path to gender equality must be built on the remains of the "throbbing lives" that have been thrown into darkness.

Indeed, as noted previously, images of suffering female bodies being thrown into a pit appeared not only in Caird's text but in the world she lived in. Between August 31 and November 9 of 1888, the prostitutes Polly Nicholls, Annie Chapman, Catherine Eddowes, Elizabeth Stride, and Mary Jane Kelly were all brutally murdered, sexually mutilated, and left in doorways, courtyards, or pathetic back rooms of the East End.[5] During the 1880s, Whitechapel was associated with problems of poverty, starvation, overcrowding, and unemployment, as well as with populations of Jews, immigrants, and refugees. Despite its name, it was imagined as a "dark" place, both literally and figuratively. For many middle and upper class readers, the sensational quality of the Ripper murders was heightened simply by the fact that they took place in Whitechapel, a locale often equated with depravity, sex, and danger.[6] In the fall of 1888, for readers who devoured stories of one murder after another after another, there may very well have seemed to be a mounting array of women's bodies in the dark pits of lower London.

Caird herself had an indirect link to the public discussion of these murders, as she herself was catapulted into fame in early August of 1888, when her article "Marriage" was published in the *Westminster Review*. The thesis of the piece, that marriage was a "vexatious failure," sent the public into an uproar. Caird's theme was consequently picked up by the *Daily Telegraph* which opened a letters column entitled "Is Marriage a Failure?" Nearly 27,000 letters were received in response (Gullette 493-95). A lively and public debate ensued in the pages of the paper and continued on until late September, when the newspaper began to focus exclusively on the Ripper murders taking place in Whitechapel. Before this shift in focus however, pieces on the two subjects (the marriage debate and the East End murders) appeared for four weeks beside one another. Consequently, discussions of the ways in which women were oppressed by the institution of marriage were juxtaposed with reports of the ways in which specific prostitutes had been murdered by an unseen but decidedly evil man.

The Ripper murders were shocking, sadistic, and misogynist. Taking place between 1888 and 1891, they presented British readers with repeated images of women's bodies, mutilated in frightening and mysterious ways. Indeed, many readers "committed to the 'medical theory'" believed that "the uterus and other internal organs were deliberately removed, while the woman's insides were often strewn about" (Walkowitz 198). These crimes were inscrutable and horrific, yet the mangled bodies of the victims came to symbolize a number of cultural ideas about the wages of sin, about the dangers of medical violence, about the potential brutality of men, and about the general victimization of women (Walkowitz). It is important, then, to postulate about what effect these images had on women readers (and perhaps on Caird herself).

Although the Ripper story most obviously became a sort of "cautionary tale" for women, warning them of the dangers that lay in immoral behavior or, more simply, in going out of doors and away from the home (Walkowitz 3), it also inspired a critique of the various ways in which all women were victimized. Judith Walkowitz notes that a number of women had been participating in critiques of male physical and sexual violence before the murders began:

> In the two decades prior to the Ripper murders, female reformers had actively engaged in public discussions of sexual danger. Through the feminist politics of prostitution, middle-class women inserted themselves into the public discussion of sex to an unprecedented extent, using access to new public spaces and to new journalistic practices to speak out against men's double lives, their sexual diseases, and their complicity in a system of vices that flourished in the undergrowth of respectable society. Along with female antivivisectionists, who plastered the thoroughfares of London with the posters of mutilated and tortured bodies of innocent "feminized" laboratory animals, feminist opponents of regulated prostitution disseminated images and narratives of scientific sexual violence [...]. These campaigns facilitated middle-class women's forceful entry into the world of publicity and politics, where they claimed themselves as part of a public that made sense of itself through public discourse. (6-7)

Despite the gruesome scenes of mutilated women's bodies – or perhaps because of them – women continued the sorts of protests described above. The horrific, pathetic state of the dead women's bodies demanded some sort of response, be it police efforts to stop the criminal or written critiques of a society that could produce such a killer.

Over the course of the 1890s, the oppression of women became an even more popular topic of public debate. As essayist A.G.P. Sykes observed in 1895, "It is not possible to ride by road or rail, to read a review, a magazine or a newspaper, without being continually reminded of ... the Woman Question" (396). Dozens of articles (critical and celebratory) about the "New Woman," the "revolting daughters," and "The Woman Question" appeared in the periodical press during the last decade of the century; in addition to these written works on the subject, Angelique

Richardson and Chris Willis claim that over a hundred novels were written about the New Woman in the years between 1883 and 1900 (1). The public fascination with the misogynistic Ripper murders and with the published work on the New Woman shows evidence of a growing interest in narratives about women's subjugation.

In the next decade, additional narratives on this topic would arise, some notably from the East End. It is interesting for the purposes of my argument to note that Sylvia Pankhurst founded the East London Federation of the Women's Social and Political Union in 1913 and that this group in particular was organized and run from the same geographical locale where the Ripper murders had occurred a quarter of a century previously. Peter Ackroyd writes, "The history of the suffragettes connected with Sylvia Pankhurst was associated very closely with that of the East End, and became a genuine expression of the area's concerns. [...] The significance of the topography of the women's movement has never adequately been analyzed, but it has become clear that the eastern areas of London lent power and authority to it" (*London* 624). In the same section of the city that had once threatened women with horrific violence, women came to campaign, in new and striking ways, for the vote and for social change.[7]

It is my argument that the nineteenth century scholar may turn from the murders at the end of the 1880s and see again the torture and brutalization of women, this time at the start of the twentieth century, as suffragettes embraced physical suffering as a meaningful form of social protest. In October 1903, Emmeline Pankhurst, along with her daughters Christabel and Sylvia, founded the Women's Social and Political Union (WSPU), a branch of the early twentieth-century women's movement that became notorious for its militant policies and whose members were the first to be christened "suffragettes." The W.S.P.U. proposed to "wake up the nation" to the issue of women's suffrage through "Deeds not Words" ("Women's Social and Political Union (WSPU)"). Women of the WSPU (as well as other female protestors) purposely endured incarceration, hunger strikes, and various other forms of physical abuse as they protested the legal and social positions of women. In addition to challenging cabinet members at public meetings, they staged demonstrations, chained their wrists to the doorknobs of public buildings, and set fire to postboxes, thus frequently inspiring the police to attack or arrest them. [8] Perhaps the most dramatic example of this sort of tactic can be seen in the actions of Emily Davison who, in 1913, threw herself under the King's horse at the Derby (in protest of the government's continued failure to grant women the vote) and who was consequently killed.

Between 1903 and the first World War, over a thousand suffragettes (including Emmeline, Christabel, Sylvia, and Adela Pankhurst) were placed in prison for their actions ("Women's Social and Political Union (WSPU)"). Many were sent to Holloway Jail in North London where they protested against prison conditions by refusing to eat ("Women's Social and Political Union (WSPU)"). Such "hunger strikes" often were met by the brutal practice of force feeding, where a rubber tube was inserted into the nose and liquidized food was pumped down it. Often women were placed in straightjackets during the process. This painful ordeal often was equated with rape by those who experienced it (Peterson 112).

Certainly the powerful public spectacle that arose from the actions of these women was one the British government appears to have been eager to suppress. Starved or force-fed bodies won authority in the public sphere; they became an "embarrassing political problem", causing many to feel sympathy for the suffragettes and distrust of the authorities ("Cat and Mouse Act"). As Herbert Asquith's Liberal Government wished to keep female protestors from becoming martyrs for their cause, the "Prisoner's Temporary Discharge of Ill Health Act" was introduced in 1913. This Act allowed suffragettes to go on hunger strike, but, once they began to exhibit signs of ill health, they would be released. Once a released prisoner had recovered, the police would re-arrest her and return her to prison, where she would complete her sentence. This method of dealing with hunger strikes became known as the "Cat and Mouse Act" (Rowbotham). Certainly the existence of this Act is evidence for how powerful a woman's choice to starve herself could be. Indeed, such purposeful destruction of individual bodies (for the sake of giving voice to larger social inequalities) inspired extensive legislation and unusual, time-consuming efforts on the part of law enforcement. It also brought attention to these women and their cause, inspiring public awareness, if not public support.

It should be noted that while the early twentieth-century suffragette movement in Britain owed a great deal both to the suffrage organizations of working-class women and to the constitutional-liberal suffragists (the NUWSS), it is unclear how successful the women of the WSPU were in their efforts to bring about votes for women.[9] As Shirley Peterson notes,

> Historians concur as to the superior visibility of the militant suffragettes, yet there is little consensus as to whether the WSPU [...] advanced or retarded the progress of the campaign during the period just before World War I. While riveting public attention to the women's cause, WSPU violence no doubt partially eroded Liberal Party support for the Conciliation Bill" (109).

A number of feminist historians have argued that this may very well have been a result of the group's more general emphasis on violent behavior. The women of the WSPU were not focused solely on highlighting the injustice of their own suffering, but also were invested in aggressive protest projects, and specifically in arson. Nevertheless, as A.N. Wilson writes,

> In his smug history of this decade, *The Edwardians*, J.B. Priestley says that the "militant" wing of the feminist movement, by their "extreme" behavior, actually delayed the arrival of Votes for Women. In a somewhat similar vein, it is suggested that if only the blacks, or the Irish, had been patient enough to trust their lords and masters, they would have been given their independence all in good time. Others, whatever their view of trouble, by whomsoever it is made, will rather doubt this. (59)

Indeed, the WSPU's dramatization of the issue seems a crucial part of the Women's Movement. Many were shocked and disturbed by the ways in which well-educated, middle-class, and (at least in the cases of Christabel Pankhurst and Annie Kenney) beautiful women endured starvation, force-feeding, and captivity.[10] Wilson writes, "As the heroines of the movement chained themselves to railings, broke shop windows, waved flags in the faces of pompous politicians, thousands of women, in quiet homes and provincial towns, joined Mrs. Pankhurst's Women's Social and Political Union" (61).

As Karlyn Kohrs Campbell has noted, "[b]ecause confrontation compels audience members to consider an issue, however distasteful that may be, it can be persuasive" (172). Even Millicent Garrett Fawcett recognized the importance of the "militant movement"; in 1912 she wrote:

> by adopting novel and startling methods [...] they succeeded in drawing a far larger amount of public attention to the claims of women to representation than ever had been given to the subject before. These methods were regarded by many suffragists with strong aversion, while others watched them with sympathy and admiration for the courage and self-sacrifice which these new methods involved. [...] Their courage made a very deep impression on the public and touched the imagination of the whole country. (30)

The ability of suffering to make a "very deep impression" and to inspire the "imagination of the whole country" is significant. In *The Daughters of Danaus*, Caird indicates that such a spectacle is needed, that the mere presentation of a just cause is not enough. At one point in the novel Lady Engleton asks a local man, "What would you say, Dodge, if some tiresome, reasonable person were to come and point out something to you that you couldn't honestly deny, and yet that seemed to upset all the ideas that you had felt were truest and best?" (261). Dodge responds that he would at first deny the information and then ignore the person, to which Hadria responds, "Dodge, you really are an oracle! [...] What could more simply describe the action of our Great Majority?" (261). This concept reappears ten years after the publication of Caird's novel: for the women of the WSPU, The Great Majority demanded not just words, but deeds. And, as Wilson notes, they may have been correct in their assumptions, for "political action became evident in the chamber of Parliament only after very disruptive action was taken on the ground by the 'militants'" (60).

Nevertheless, despite their moving successes, it should not be forgotten that the political strategies of the WSPU were terribly damaging to the bodies of individual women. Many suffragettes never really recovered from prison, hunger strikes and force feeding. In this and in Caird's novel, suffering, while it draws the attention and sympathy of others, can destroy the body of the injured woman. As Kenneth O. Morgan notes, the WSPU "inflict[ed] through imprisonment and hunger strikes considerable hardship and even occasionally death upon its members" (577). In history and in fiction, the price of liberty is high for the individual woman who feels compelled to fight for it.

It is interesting to note how Caird's 1894 novel is poised between these two real life examples of violence against women (the Ripper murders of 1888-91 and the suffering suffragettes of the first decade of the nineteenth century). Just as Caird shows readers how an author might write about women in such a way that refrains from either showing once transgressive heroines finally resigned to a domestic sphere (as Angelica in Sarah Grand's *The Heavenly Twins*) or dead (as Lyndall in Olive Schreiner's *The Story of an African Farm*), her presentation of meaningful suffering may have helped to give rise to the ways that living women protested the conditions of their lives. The women murdered by Jack the Ripper left behind bodies that were mysteriously, tragically destroyed. Caird's heroine watches her health fade in a way that is less obviously horrific, yet she is determined to note the damage and speak openly about its cause. Consequently, *The Daughters of Danaus*, in its recognition of the suffering of bourgeois, educated, married women, required readers to reformulate cultural ideas about all women. Its emphasis on such suffering called traditional methods of social categorization into question, drawing attention to the damage caused by the conditions of "normal" women's lives. The image of the suffering woman is transformed in Caird's novel; we see dead bodies thrown carelessly into a pit, but we also see a woman who explores and protests her own suffering. Thus, in addition to reworking novelistic traditions that left major characters dead or married, one might perhaps hypothesize that the surviving, suffering heroine Hadria looks forward to the ways that the members of the twentieth century's women's movement suffered vocally, meaningfully, and productively. Indeed, it may be the harm they inflicted onto their own bodies that has allowed women of the twenty and twenty-first centuries to begin to venture over the dark pit of gender discrimination. We stand on their backs.

Works Cited

Ackroyd, Peter, ed. *Jack the Ripper and the East End*. London: Chatto and Windus, 2008.
—. *London: The Biography*. 2000. London: Anchor, 2003.
Baumeister, Roy F. *Masochism and the Self*. New Jersey: Lawrence Erlbaum Associates, 1989.
Brandon, Ruth. *The New Woman and the Old Men: Love, Sex, and the Woman Question*. London: Secker and Warburg, 1990.
Caird, Mona. *The Daughters of Danaus*. New York: The Feminist Press, 1989.
—. "A Defense of the So-Called 'Wild Women.'" *Nineteenth Century* 31 (1892): 811-829.
—. "Marriage." *Westminster Review* 130:2 (August 1888): 186-201.
—. *The Wing of Azrael*. London: Trubner & Co., 1889.
Campbell, Karlyn Kohrs. *Man Cannot Speak for Her: A Critical Study of Early Feminist Rhetoric, Volume 1*. New York: Praeger, 1989.
"Cat and Mouse Act." *Microsoft Encarta Online Encyclopedia* 2008. 27 July 2008 <http://uk.encarta.msn.com>.
Cowman, Krista. *Women of the Right Spirit: Paid Organizers of the Women's Social and Political Union (WSPU), 1904-18*. Manchester: Manchester UP, 2007.
Davis, Mary. *About Sylvia Pankhurst*. The Sylvia Pankhurst Memorial Committee. 27 July 2003. 28 July 2008 <http://sylviapankhurst.gn.apc.org/sylvia.htm>.
Deleuze, Gilles. *Masochism: Coldness and Cruelty*. New York: Zone Books, 1989.
Fawcett, Millicent Garrett. "The Militant Societies," *Literature of the Women's Suffrage Campaign in England*. Ed. Carolyn Christensen Nelson (New York: Broadview Press, 2004).
Felski, Rita. *The Gender of Modernity*. Cambridge, MA: Harvard University Press, 1995.

Giblin, James and Dale Ferguson. *The Scarecrow Book*. New York: Crown Publishers, 1980.

Gullette, Margaret Morganroth. Afterword to *The Daughters of Danaus*. New York: The Feminist Press, 1989.

Heilmann, Ann. *New Woman Fiction: Women Writing First Wave Feminism*. New York: St. Martin's Press, 2000.

Ledger, Sally. *The New Woman: Fiction and Feminism at the Fin-de-siècle*. Manchester: Manchester UP, 1997.

Morgan, Kenneth O. *The Oxford History of Britain*. Oxford: Oxford UP, 2001.

Murphy, Patricia. *Time is of the Essence: Temporality, Gender, and the New Woman*. New York: State University of New York Press, 2001.

Noble, Marianne. *The Masochistic Pleasures of Sentimental Literature*. Princeton, NJ: Princeton UP, 2000.

Peterson, Shirley. "The Politics of a Moral Crusade: Gertrude Colmore's *Suffragette Sally*." *Rediscovering Forgotten Radicals: British Women Writers, 1889-1939*. eds. Angela Ingram and Daphne Patal. Chapel Hill, The U of NC P, 1993.

Priestley, J.B. *The Edwardians*. New York: Penguin, 2000.

Reed, John R. *Victorian Will*. Athens: Ohio UP, 1989.

Richardson, Angelique and Chris Willis. "Introduction." *The New Woman in Fiction and* in Fact: Fin-de-Siècle Feminisms. London: Palgrave, 2001.

Rowbotham, Sheila. *A Century of Women: The History of Women in Britain and the United States in the Twentieth Century*. New York: Penguin, 1997.

Smith, Harold L. *The British Women's Suffrage Campaign, 1866-1928*. London: Longman Publishing Group, 1998.

Sugden, Philip. *The Complete History of Jack the Ripper*. New York: Avalon Publishing, 2002.

Sykes, A.G.P. "The Evolution of the Sex." *Westminster Review* 143 (1895):396-400.

Walkowitz, Judith. *The City of Dreadful Delight: Narratives of Sexual Danger in Late Victorian London*. London: Virago, 1992.

Wendell, Susan. *The Rejected Body: Feminist Philosophical Reflections on Disability*. New York: Rutledge, 1996.

Wilson, A.N. *After the Victorians: the Decline of Britain in the World*. New York: Picador, 2005.

"Women's Social and Political Union (WSPU)." *Exploring 20ᵗʰ Century London.* Museum of London 27 July 2008 <http://www.20thcenturylondon.org.uk/server.php?show=conInformationRecord.271.>.

Notes

[1] The Married Woman's Property Acts of 1870 and 1882 allowed women to own property independently of their husbands; the Infants Bill of 1886 recognized the mother as the natural guardian of her children on the death of the father; the Separation and Maintenance Act of 1895 allowed magistrates to grant custody of children to the wife rather than to the husband in cases of marital breakdown.

[2] Interestingly, the fiftieth daughter of Danaus, Hypermestra, spared her husband Lynceus. Significantly, the descendents of this pair are Perseus (who grows up to kill Medusa) and two princesses who go mad and roam the countryside, thinking they are cows.

[3] In Greek mythology, the shirt of Nessus has been poisoned with the tainted blood of the centaur Nessus. Hercules' wife, Deiarenia, unknowingly gives this cursed gift to Hercules, burning him, and driving him to throw himself onto a funeral pyre.

[4] Certainly one kind of "scarecrow" is the criminal body; the straw man hanging in the fields bears a certain resemblance to the dead man hanging on the gibbets, a gruesome reminder of state power, designed to scare a populace into docility. Yet despite this, scarecrows also can be associated with the land and the people that work it. In Charles Dickens's 1859 work *A Tale of Two Cities*, Dickens describes the pre-mob populace of Paris as "scarecrows", calling forth an image of seemingly innocuous watchers in rags, waiting for their moment to rise up against their oppressors. Finally, the scarecrow can be interpreted as a sort of Christ figure, reminiscent of the innocent God who was crucified on the cross in order to atone for the sins of others.

[5] For an excellent discussion of the details of the events, rather than an exploration of a theory or particular suspect, see Philip Sugden's *The Complete History of Jack the Ripper.*

[6] For additional analyses of the public's perceptions of Whitechapel, see *Jack the Ripper and the East End.*

[7] This suffragettes in the East End fought for the vote even when other women gave up the cause. According to Mary Davis, "Sylvia's strategy, which linked class and gender, did not find favour with the most famous of the suffragette organisations, the Women's Social and Political Union (WSPU), to which she belonged and to which the East London Federation was affiliated. [...] Sylvia was expelled [...] from the WSPU in 1914. The WSPU abandoned its early links with the labour movement in 1907 and in 1914, with the outbreak of World War One, it abandoned the suffrage campaign itself. Emmeline and Christabel Pankhurst

ardently supported the war effort and urged all women to do the same. Sylvia did not take their advice. Her organization was one of the very few to maintain the fight for the vote."

[8] For more information on the specific women who ran the organization and the protests they organized, see Krista Cowman, *Women of the Right Spirit: Paid Organizers of the Women's Social and Political Union (WSPU), 1904-18.*

[9] The National Union of Women's Suffrage Societies (NUWSS) was founded by Millicent Fawcett in 1897 and is generally credited with getting women (over the age of thirty) the vote in 1918. According to Kenneth O. Morgan, it "unit[ed] [...] a number of well-established organizations, [and] was a broadly based movement of impeccably liberal credentials which made considerable headway. It was, however, outflanked and outshone by the Pankhursts' Women's Social and Political Union" (577). For more information on the long history of women's groups and their efforts to achieve suffrage, see *The British Women's Suffrage Campaign, 1866-1928* by Harold L. Smith.

[10] Wilson writes, "Christabel and Annie Kenney made a splendid pair. Christabel had a marvelous speaking voice and beautiful skin. Annie, more abrasive and Yorkshire, had fair hair and blazing blue eyes" (60).

CHAPTER FIVE

READING BOOKS AND BODY:
NEW WOMAN AND AUTHORITY

DONNA DECKER

In 1898, George Egerton rewrote Charlotte Brontë's *Jane Eyre* (1847). *The Wheel of God* (1898) is a reply to Brontë's feminist cult novel that "writes beyond the romantic ending"of Brontë's marriage plot, retelling the text as a New Woman novel with an all-female communal ending.[1] Neither female authority nor mid-nineteenth-century narrative possibilities could allow Brontë to take her protagonist where Egerton takes her Mary Desmond. The counter-narratives open to New Woman writers, fifty years after Brontë's novel, represent the "prodigious amount of talking [it takes] to get an idea into the world's brain."[2]

Egerton, like Brontë, imbued her heroine with the authority that comes from the lived experience of reading critically both male bodies and books.[3] This repeated practice of textual analysis translates into the heroines' authority to frame their own judgment regarding embodied patriarchy. The *fin de siecle* was a time of deep concern about bodies. If in the earlier Victorian era, "men's bodies were often taken to be unmarked sites of political, economic, and sexual subjectivity," (Cohen qtd. In Michie 412) then new woman novels beg the question of what these male bodies *do* to "earn" the authority they wield. They demystify the male body and its attendant privilege.

When *Jane Eyre* was published in 1847, no university in England was open to women. Nevertheless, women were dialogically active in both the international women's movement and on the literary front.[4] Bonnie S. Anderson calls the time between Brontë's and Egerton's novels "the heyday" of international feminism.[5]

Laws affecting the position of women – including those concerned with divorce, custody, battering and rape – exhibit a trend, from the beginning to the end of the nineteenth century, away from physical violence in the conjugal relationship. Male power was being redefined, then, in relation to women's bodies as well as to men's bodies (Michie 415)[6].

The New Woman was, arguably, the avatar of this collective women's activism. A contested historical figure of the late nineteenth century, the New Woman was white, well-educated, middle-class, and openly-critical of traditional gender roles, particularly roles that demand a wife leave work or art behind to serve husband and home. Influenced by contemporary activist women, the New Woman was making a significant move from the private to the public sphere. She signified the antithesis of the Victorian "angel in the house," giving voice "to what other people [were] only daring to think" (Sarah Grand qtd. in S. Mitchell ix). Over one hundred novels about the New Woman were written during the last quarter (between 1883 -1900) of the nineteenth century (Ardis 4). Many of these explicitly attack marriage as a hegemonic tool of patriarchy, an institution women should avoid until it is renovated. I argue that with the heft of fifty years of both legislative authority and feminist dialogue about the Woman Question behind her, Egerton offers not only an alternative to heterosexual marriage for heroines like Jane Eyre, but she examines the means by which heroines come to claim the authority to embrace such alternatives.

The cultural work that Egerton is able to do in proposing an all-female communal ending is to challenge the

> limits of what will and will not be called reality. Fantasy is what allows us
> to imagine ourselves and others otherwise; it establishes the possible in
> excess of the real; it points elsewhere, and when it is embodied, it brings
> the elsewhere home. (Butler, *Undoing* 29)

Embodying patriarchy in male characters who are known by the heroines and urging heroines to read them as texts functions pedagogically to illustrate patriarchy and its effects: "New Woman novels are presented as agents of change" (Richardson, "Allopathic" 15), with a vision of the possible.

New Woman scholarship claims George Egerton as one of its central writers. Mary Chavelita Dunne Golding Bright Clairmonte (1859-1945), who derived her penname from the name of her husband George Egerton Clairmonte, however, would be as appalled today to find herself discussed as a New Woman writer as she was when she learned of herself hailed as the new Olive Schreiner or Sarah Grand (Stetz, "George" 67).[7] Though she dissociates herself here and elsewhere from feminist activism, she very decidedly does the cultural work of such activism in her fiction. In *Rosa Amorosa*, she writes:

> Why should you or I accept any man's *ipse dixit* as final? If he is an
> authority on some special subject about which you know nothing, listen to
> him with respect, because he may be right; and, in any case, you don't
> know enough to contradict him; but take no man's opinion on questions of
> right or wrong for you individually, on subjects of which you have ample
> opportunity in your daily life of framing your own judgment. (133)[8]

This framing of one's own judgment is what interests Egerton. Woman's
"development from within out as a female, that woman …has begun to tell
the truth about herself, or at least the half truth" (Egerton, *Rosa Amorosa*
140). The only way to get at such truth, reminds Dale Bauer, is to "learn a
persuasive inner speech by reading [the] present situation and revising the
notions which she inherits from her parents and her society" (*Feminist*
118).

Egerton's rewrite of *Jane Eyre* retains the reading heroine who revises
what she finds in books and bodies. In *The Wheel of God,* Egerton tells the
story of an Irish girl, Mary Desmond, who lives with her ill mother and her
siblings. Her father, Major Desmond, lives a hedonistic lifestyle in
Marshalsea debtors' prison where the community of men in the prison
drinks and eats well, gambles, and shirks familial responsibility. As the
oldest child in the Desmond family, Mary takes responsibility for bringing
home money and food. Despite her best efforts, Mary's mother and one
sibling die. The Major, upon release from prison, does little more to
support the remaining family than he did while in prison. As a young
adult, Mary sails to America to earn a living in a factory. Where she grew
up in a world dominated by males, in America she is introduced to a
boardinghouse world populated by women working to earn their own
livings. It is a lonely and disillusioning world, and Mary eventually returns
to live in London where her father has settled. Her first brief marriage is to
the terminally ill D'Arcy. Her second marriage is to a prodigal doctor
named Cecil Marriott whose narcissism wearies Mary. With this husband,
she has a baby girl. The child dies within three days. Despite Egerton's
insistence that Mary Desmond yearns for love, we do not see Mary
Desmond through the lens of the romance plot or the traditional marriage
plot. In fact, the love for which Mary yearns remains unfulfilled in
heterosexual romance. While Mary does marry twice, these marriages are
positioned in the middle of the narrative rather than at the end. She settles
into a life of disillusionment and loneliness until such time as she meets
several intellectually vibrant women with whom she develops intimate
friendships that serve to fulfill her lifelong yearning for love.

Egerton is clearly more ambivalent about the possibilities of success in
marriage than is Brontë. Brontë's Jane settles into a heterosexual family at

the end of the novel, her "unregenerate spirit" folded into hetero-normativity. Mary Desmond, nearly supine from ennui and chronic bad male behavior, is revived at the end of her novel to nest in a homosocial intellectual community of women, heeding and echoing the warning that women should eschew marriage until the institution is renovated.[9] While fifty years bore witness to much cultural and gender change in England, it did not sufficiently renovate marriage to the satisfaction of many New Woman novelists who continued to argue, in dialogue with each other and their opponents, in polemical fiction and in polemical non-fiction, that it is "a vexatious failure."[10] Egerton "selectively assimilates the words," of Brontë, not only "retelling [Brontë's] text in [her] own words" (Bakhtin, *DI* 341), but assuming responsibility for the future of the New Woman. To take such an authoritative step, according to Judith Butler, "is not to know its direction fully in advance, since the future, especially the future with and for others, requires a certain openness and unknowingness" (Butler, *Undoing* 39).[11] Egerton takes that risk.

Russian critic Mikhail Bakhtin's theory of discourse in the novel best allows me to read these two fictions in dialogue with one another across an historical span of half a century.[12] More specifically, Bakhtinian theory employed by feminist theorists Dale Bauer and Teresa Mangum enables my case.[13] Bakhtin's focus on marginalized voices within hegemonic power structures makes the application of his theory to the case of women ideal.[14]

For New Women heroines, in particular, reading books is one of the earliest acts of dialogue with other minds.[15] One might argue, at least metaphorically, that the very survival of the New Woman depends on reading. Teresa Mangum contends in *Married, Middlebrow, and Militant,* that

> The New Woman must learn first and foremost to be a critic of her culture. Her failure or success depends on how well she learns to read – men's books, men's reasoning, men's means of control, and the masculine privilege that organizes the marriage plot (90).[16]

The repeated act of reading functions to hone a reader's ability to interpret another's point of view.

It does more than this, however. The act of reading hones the ability to interpret other forms of texts or other forms that can be read and interpreted as texts (symbolic analysis). In this reading, I demonstrate that human bodies are read, as texts, by the heroines. In essence, this position takes Mangum's exhortation to read men's books, reasoning, and privilege one step further to reading human bodies: both men's bodies and the effects of men's books, reasoning, and privilege on female bodies. In other words, in order for Jane and Mary to claim authority over their own destinies, they must learn to read the bodies of male characters as embodiments of patriarchy and female bodies as disciplined by that patriarchy.[17]

For the discriminating reader, Dale Bauer argues, there "is an education in [what Bakhtin calls] misreading...especially when that misunderstanding unmasks the power structures which enforce conformity" (160). The misunderstanding character, explains Bauer, functions to "defamiliarize the conventions which have been accepted as 'natural'" (*Feminist* 13).[18] Reading bodies as texts calls for such discrimination (and misreading), as well, allowing the protagonists to recognize embodied patriarchy, to distinguish between what those bodies say and what those bodies do. How else does one learn to recognize where oppression comes from? How authority accrues to some bodies and not others? Honing this type of analytical reading is the groundwork that must be laid in order to earn the authority to resist and question. Because she reads books, Mary Desmond discovers that authoritative discourses are not self-evident truths but rather perspectives on the world that are constructed and bolstered by power. Both Jane Eyre and Mary Desmond come by their authority to make judgments about their adult lives by reading in this way. Each novelist creates a protagonist with enough intellectual acuity and enough heartfelt disillusionment with normative experiences of love and romance to be ready to embrace a new way.

That embryonic character is introduced as the reading child.[19] What Egerton creates in the opening chapter of *The Wheel of God* is a fecund intellectual and aesthetic athenaeum: "the old nursery of her father's home" (3) in which the child can maximize her engagement with other minds. That nursery becomes the site of her earliest dialogue with ideas, and Egerton suffuses that world with dozens of book and periodical titles. The heroines Mary "acts out" are representations of women by men – the very thing Egerton is committed to work against. "I realised," says George Egerton in *Ten Contemporaries* (1932),

> that in literature, everything had been better done by man than woman
> could hope to emulate. There was only one small plot left for her to tell:
> the *terra incognita* of herself, as she knew herself to be, not as man liked
> to imagine her (58).

Acting out enables Mary to try on (embody) the text of women disciplined by or resistant to patriarchy. Before Mary can read, or even write, the *terra incognita* of herself, she must learn to read others. Egerton frames her reading in complex ways, studded with canonical males but ballasted on either end with women writers: Mary reads Charlotte Brontë at the beginning of the novel and "John Morton," the pen name used by a female character who enters the novel late, at the end.

Both *Jane Eyre* and *The Wheel of God* open with a scene of reading.[20] In close proximity to those initial scenes of reading in the novels are scenes of rage at men who embody patriarchy. Even as children, both Jane and Mary misread male bodies. That is, they question and resist male authority, comparing men's visions of self to "gods" and "Roman Emperors" (Brontë 8) but clearly not accepting these positions as credible All in all, at Gateshead and Lowood, young Jane must learn to read three male bodies to young Mary's one in Ireland: the violent John Reed, the nurturing Mr. Lloyd, and the pretentious Mr. Brocklehurst. Jane reads John Reed as "not quick either of vision or conception" (7) and "large and stout for his age, with a dingy and unwholesome skin; thick lineaments in a spacious visage, heavy limbs and large extremities. He gorged himself habitually at table, which made him bilious, and gave him a dim and bleared eye and flabby cheeks" (7). Reed scorns females; he bullies and strikes Jane. Jane's response to her cousin is one of visceral repugnance; "every morsel of flesh on my bones shrank when he came near" (8). Jane admits that that while she longed for "escape from insurmountable oppression," it took her "many years" to see her "vassalage" clearly (12). Had she been a body who endured her oppression quietly, Jane might have suffered less. Reed's bullying is his means of asserting patriarchy; it is, perhaps, the most elemental or vulgar presentation of patriarchy. Bullying turns to violence as power's last resort when its victim refuses victimization. Jane aptly misreads her "vassalage" to her cousin clearly as the consequence, in part, of Reed's unearned privilege of primogeniture that "authorizes" his boorishness.

As a counterpoint to John Reed's patriarchy, Jane learns that men *can* assert power without force. Mr. Lloyd, the apothecary, is a kind man who sees Jane's situation clearly, who has a "good-natured looking face" (19) and sits "in the chair near [her] pillow" (15), and arranges her to move away from one oppressor. Lloyd. Lloyd has the authority to resist Jane's legal guardian because of his professional position, open at this time only to men.

Mr. Brocklehurst embodies phallic hegemony:

—a black pillar! such, at least, appeared to me, at first sight, the straight, narrow, sable-clad shape standing erect on the rug: the grim face at the top was like a carved mask, placed above the shaft by way of capital" (26).

Despite this odious image, Jane misreads Brocklehurst a few paragraphs later: "What a face he had, now that it was almost on a level with mine! What a great nose! and what a mouth! and what large prominent teeth!" (26). If Jane is unequivocal in her description of Brocklehurst as staunchly male, in the first quotation, she is mocking in her assessment of him as a fairy tale villain, in the second, reducing his power by misreading it as comic. Brontë demonstrates Jane's authority in reading Brocklehurst's brand of patriarchy by infusing her lines with humor. This allows her the distance from power to assess it, rather than accept it. Pages later, she refers to Brocklehurst as a "piece of architecture...longer, narrower, and more rigid than ever" (52). Her persistent invocation of phallic metaphor to read Brocklehurst suggests her growing acumen in symbolic analysis. Patriarchal authority embodied as it is in a character like Brocklehurst, is the easiest to recognize: haughty, convinced of its self-evident importance, what Bakhtin calls authoritative or monologic, almost a parody of itself.

As Jane and Mary are developing their critical abilities to read embodied patriarchy, their own bodies are disciplined by that patriarchy. Jane is "ill," (19), "knocked down" (19), "physically weak and broken down" (16), with an "unutterable wretchedness of mind" (16). Mary Desmond is "anemic" (Egerton 40), "not robust" (51), "cold, sick" (47), with "bloodless lips" (51). In the *Wheel of God,* inside Marshalsea prison where female prisoners cook and clean for male prisoners, who have escaped wives and families (23), Mary Desmond visits her father in his "very cosy room" (14) with its "gay rug," "Indian screen that hid a bath" (14), and an easel near the window. Mary sees the enormous kitchen with glowing grill with its hedonistic culinary display, rich with venison, game, fowl, and vegetables. In her father's room, half a dozen men smoked and drank whiskey. One prisoner wears a beflowered dressing gown and Turkish fez (14). Laughter abounds and canaries sing (13), and there is even a racket court and tinkley piano. With a resolute face and poised head, Mary listens as her father claims himself helpless to pay to feed his family at home. Mary does not say aloud what she thinks, but she reads the prison population clearly: the women her father knows in prison, she concludes, are "bigoted, with shrines for little conventional gods erected in their souls" (25), and the men are "curious things...like children...they seemed to have no real sense...they made such a fuss about small things, and yet they let important things go by. She could not imagine grown-up women playing the fool, as she had seen men do" (25-26).

Mary estimates she would "not marry when she grew up; she would paint, and stay with the mother" (26). She accurately reads her father as shirking his familial responsibilities and endangering the well-being of his family. The consequence for Mary is that she becomes the mother figure; her own mother is dying, and in their last scene together, their bodies metaphorically meld into "the child-woman and woman-child" (28). Her visit to the prison affirms her reading of the type of men and women she rejects as role models. Patriarchy that asserts its rights but neglects its responsibilities repels her. For Mary, the indulgences of her father's male body cost her own and her mother's female bodies dearly.

As she does in reading Marshalsea's male bodies, Mary resists orthodox readings of canonical male texts. Like other New Woman protagonists, she engages such authoritative discourses with inquisitiveness and sometimes irreverence. Mary mis-reads more than she reads men's reasoning within these texts. The received wisdom of such texts befuddles Mary. For example, she reads the Bible as a child, and she loves the baby Jesus because he is pink and cute. But she finds the grown Jesus "stupid" (Egerton 8). Why come as a carpenter's son when he might have come as a ruler with power and have made the world happy? Consistently, she resists readings of men as respectable leaders to whom women should look up. Mary's quandary takes the form of primal rage later on in her childhood, long before she can express it in dialogue with another. At several moments of extreme resistance to authority, Mary holds her tongue. When her mother dies, Mary does not speak. Rather, she "had bitten her wrist till her teeth drew blood, in her effort to conquer the inclination" (32). At her confirmation, she longs to cry out, "It is sacrilege which I am about to do; I don't believe any of it" (101). She says nothing, however. Mary's suffering from a rage against authority that cannot yet be voiced indicates a teeming inner life that serves as prerequisite for dialogic interaction with authority.[21] And her rage is unable yet to be directed outward but at her own body. What the youthful Mary gains from reading books and from reading her own experience with men is what Jane learns: to recognize what patriarchy looks like and acts like and how male privilege is girded by systemic complicity.

Whereas Mary Desmond encounters very few women in her early years, Jane Eyre meets with two at Lowood who serve to embody significant textual lessons: Miss Temple and Helen Burns. Miss Maria Temple is a fashionable and "refined" teacher, whose physical descriptions include a pale and clear complexion, a stately air and carriage. The student body rises "simultaneously" (39) when Miss Temple enters, and she is met with universal respect and awe. Temple is "pale as marble," a veritable human shrine. It is her mission to counter the patriarchy of Brocklehurst. Where he intends to starve the bodies of the female students at Lowood, to save their souls, Temple feeds them. When their breakfast is untenable one morning, she feeds them bread and cheese. When Jane has been punished and humiliated by Brocklehurst, Temple serves tea in china cups along with special seed cakes (61). Temple claims what authority she can to save the bodies of her students. She is "mother, governess, companion" (73) to Jane until "destiny in the shape of the Reverend Mr. Nasmyth came between [Jane] and Miss Temple" (73). Ultimately, Temple's power is a bandaid on the hurt female body. She escapes Lowood via marriage, leaving Jane alone to yearn for a new servitude.

Though she is but fourteen, Helen Burns has a suffering body and dies of consumption after a few short scenes. Nevertheless, she serves, ironically, to foreground the Christian ideal of the afterlife, "eternal rest" (50), death as the "entrance to glory" (59). Burns's philosophy echoes that of early Christians for whom the new religion held immense appeal in that it acknowledged that for some, human happiness is elusive (41), and so held out hope for the possibility of an afterlife, a promise long dangled by power over the weak. Jane reads Helen as wise and strong and mysterious, though she cannot abide her philosophy. In a singularly poignant tableau, the two girls lie entwined in each other's arms in Helen's crib in Miss Temple's room, the one dead, the other alive: twin female bodies, predictive of Jane and Bertha's inevitable twinning.

Helen Burns and Miss Temple serve as female bodies who are disciplined by patriarchy. Reading them as texts, Jane sees the machinations each must engage in order to exert what authority they can – impotent though it be – to help Jane, Helen by offering hope and love, Temple sustenance for the body. Helen's docile body inhabits a textual world of intellect and religion, a gnosis that permits her to abide (not resist) until a better world arrives. Temple's ministrations are healing but inadequate in a sphere so totalized by patriarchy.

Both Jane and Mary escape from scarring childhood patriarchy on entering the workforce. They now must support their own bodies by working. Jane finds her "new servitude" at Thornfield, and Mary finds work in American and then London. They enter their early adulthood with budding ideologies of their own, extrapolated from their reading of bodies and books. In addition to the rejection of male posturing as deities, both heroines reject heaven as a patriarchal Christian construct created to reward the complicit, like Helen Burns. The heroines share a mutual disregard for heaven. Jane maintains Psalms are "not interesting" and can avoid hell only by not dying (27). For Mary, "heaven interested her least of all" (8). [22] Rejecting heaven though they do, both Jane and Mary seek solitude on rooftops, a liminal space in both novels between their arduous circumstances on earth and the possibilities of the unknown. An unquiet mind is a keynote of both heroines. Both find contemplative space on the roof, Jane on the roof of her place of employment, Thornfield, and Mary on the roof of her workplace in America. In *The Wheel of God*, Egerton's narrator says:

> Mary felt she could not have held out a day longer, were it not for her visits to the roof, where she drew in long breaths of the clean, strong, sea air, with the vigorous smack of spring...she could hear the sap rising in a hundred imagined trees; see the buds, and burgeons, and fronds uncurl and burst; feel all the mysterious stirring, and working into life, in the world of beast and bird; the birthing of lambs and springing of foals in the meadows. The very jiva of the earth seemed to stir in her senses, making her conscious of her womanhood in some subtle way: calling, calling, calling in her, whispering and luring in her, until her limbs ached with the stress of it, and her very soul was thirsty...Mary was realizing for the first time, one of the tragedies of her sex, her affectability; the primitive element in her, untouched by its passage through all the centuries, keeping her sib to the earth and the tings of it; closer to the forces of nature than man – genetic woman, answering to the call of the generative season. (95-96)

On the roof at Thornfield, Jane Eyre thinks:

> The restlessness was in my nature; it agitated me to pain sometimes. Then the sole relief was to walk...backwards and forwards, safe in the silence and solitude of the spot and allow my mind's eye to dwell on whatever bright visions rose before it – and, certainly, they were many and glowing; to let my heart be heaved by the exultant movement, which, while it swelled it in trouble, expanded it with life; and best of all, to open my inward ear to a tale that was never ended – a tale my imagination created, and narrated continuously; quickened with all of incident, life, fire, feeling, that I desired and had not in my actual existence...Millions are in silent revolt against their lot...Women are supposed to be very calm generally: but women feel just as men feel; they need exercise for their faculties and field for their efforts as much as their brothers do; they suffer from too rigid a restraint, to absolute an stagnation, precisely as men would suffer; and it is narrow-minded in their privileged fellow-creatures to say that they ought to confine themselves to making puddings and knitting stockings...it is thoughtless to condemn them, or laugh at them, if they seek to do more or learn more than custom has pronounced necessary for their sex. (93)

Both novels privilege the vital inner intellectual lives of their protagonists through exposing their "monologues" from on high. What Jane and Mary think and feel catalyzes the plot. Keenly sexual and revolutionary, these speeches are clearly subversive of the gendered roles expected of females.

They stand out as code for female yearning that is cast in the language of sexuality in order to infuse it with determination and energy. These are not fleeting fancies; Jane Eyre and Mary Desmond demand more from the world that what their circumstances have allowed. Embodied patriarchy has yet to quash their spunk. It has, nevertheless, clarified for Jane and Mary their understanding of themselves as part of an oppressed group; it is not their personal plight, but that of womankind, that is at stake. These are important, albeit axiomatic, realizations going into adulthood. Poised to continue reading new scenarios, Mary and Jane each meets a pair of female mentors, Jane's second set, who function to teach them further about the effects of patriarchy on women's bodies.

A young-adult Mary travels to America to work and then to London. If she knows very few women in her early life, she knows very few men in this phase. Indeed, the bodies she reads most closely as texts are those of two female co-workers, Septima and the bowmaker. Mary works with fifty women of all ages in an office building. In winter, she is cold and aching, underdressed and underfed. Mary befriends a

> girl who had interested her from the first. A pale, slight reed of a girl, delicate as an early wind-flower; eyes blue, full and soft, with the look of an appealing child. Superfinely delicate skin, with the bloom of a baby. (78)

Septima is described several more times as a baby, though paradoxically she is also of the "wild set" (78). A "racking cough" for which she keeps "paregoric in her desk" points to ill health and ultimate demise. Septima and Mary share pots of tea and treats, reminiscent of Jane's repast with Miss Temple and Helen, and they walk to and from work together since they live in the same block.

Septima's room is ultra feminine: smelling of violets, lavender silk tea-gown with ribbons and lace and silk stockings scattered about. Tiny "silver-embroidered Turkish slippers" lay on the floor. And an engraving of Dore's "Paola and Francesca de Rimini" hangs on the wall over the bed. Though Septima has "deliciously pink" cheeks and "brilliant" eyes, and a "feverishly bright" smile (81), Mary reads Septima's body as "feverish, infectious" (83) "electric, magnetic...quivering" (83). In pointedly juxtaposed scenes, Mary dreams of being taken away to a kingdom "where love reigns supreme" (97) just prior to finding Septima unconscious in her room with an empty bottle of paregoric on the floor, murmuring the name "'Carlos, Carlito'" (99). When Septima awakes, Mary lies down next to her in bed, as Jane has with Helen Burns, and Septima confesses she is in love with a married man who has a new baby. Pointing to the Dore print of the hell-bound adulterers, Septima admits she would go to hell to be with Carlos for eternity. Shortly after, when Carlos leaves Septima, Mary once again discovers Septima unconscious, this time dead from an overdose of laudanum. Septima leaves for Mary a copy of her Dante with this note: "'Love is stronger than death, for death has a limitation: death can but kill one, love may murder two'" (119). Ultra feminine Septima, caught up in an adulterous affair that is symbolically reinforced by the Dore print of adulterous lovers in hell, takes her own life. This tragedy shines an ironic light on Mary's dream of love reigning supreme. Septima does not learn to read male bodies even after Carlos admits, as does Rochester to Jane, that he married his wife because of her "glorious body" and her wealth. Septima is a naive victim of empty patriarchal promises about love.

Mary meets her second female friend, a bowmaker who lives in the same boarding house as Mary, when she moves to London after Septima's death. The bowmaker, who remains otherwise unnamed, has a body marked as aristocratic of high-born. Her voice is distinct and has careful enunciation: "she had studied to eliminate all commonness from her speech" (142), as Septima had done. The bowmaker nurtures Mary's body, providing her a footbath and felt slippers. The young woman's cubicle in the boarding house is filled with books – Bible, Carlyle, Stuart Mill, Darwin, Marcus Aurelius, a German grammar – but the bowmaker maintains that her knowledge comes from one man "'worth ten Birkbecks(University of London); [who] drew one out instead of larding one with bits of educational fat'" (143). The bowmaker tells Mary she is in love with this man, a socialist, "a man in ten thousand, a man with some of the Christ in him," (159).

"I became sacred to myself, because of the something akin to divine he awoke in me" (160), she tells Mary, "and in that supreme moment we were one complete being, soul dovetailed to soul – our wedding and renunciation in one" (160). By this she means the two love enough to marry but do not do so, in deference to his career. Bowmaker says:

> Men such as he belong to humanity...they must be celibates tied to no one woman; at the service of all suffering womanhood; father to the orphan little ones of the whole world. Families may mean holy ties, but they may also mean growths of parasitical tendency, sapping the vigour of a plant or tree. (161)

The bowmaker will never have a child, and she will never have a home with the man she loves, she acknowledges to Mary. This god-man, she insists, is worth the sacrifice. Bowmaker warns Mary, whom she calls "woman with the question in your eyes!" (162)), don't 'let the love hunger that is in you lead you to drink before the right man holds the chalice to your lips. You loving, tender thing! – better to go hungry, thirsty, and love-weaned by years of solitude to your grave – and yet – who knows? There are more ways than one of climbing the ladder to perfection'. (162)

What is Mary to make of her two friends who apotheosize the men they love, as do the women who serve men in Marshalsea prison? The first friend loves to death, the latter to a renunciation of carnal relation that she calls happiness. Though Mary is paying close attention to these "romances," she is not exonerated by these from making her own mistakes with love later on.

Before Jane can meet her next set of female mentors, she must be freed of the embodied rage of Bertha Mason. Jane Eyre leaves Thornfield and the ersatz bigamist Rochester in the night, as if heading for the "scaffold" (274).[23] Her language continues in the metaphorical vein of execution. She speaks of the "block and the axe-edge; of the disseverment of bone and vein; of the grave gaping at the end" (274), all images of splitting of the body and death. Her worry over Rochester was a "barbed arrow-head in [her]breast" (274). She is injured, wounded, and she falls, "face to the wet turf" (274), but she rises on "hands and knees," and then to her feet and moves on. By now Jane is "destitute" (275) and starving. By the end of this three-day journey, Jane is exhausted and starving, hunger a "beak and talons in my side" (279). At her lowest, she begs for porridge intended for a pig, and she eats it ravenously. Stripped of signifying signs of her position as governess and as beloved of a wealthy landowning man, reduced to animal, a nearly dead Jane arrives at Marsh End. In a pathetic tableau, Jane remains outside looking in at the "peace and warmth" (283). When she derives the courage to knock, she sinks "on the wet door-step," worn out (286).

This symbolic death and resurrection, leads Jane to assume a "new identity" in "Jane Elliott" (287), the name she gives the Rivers family. Like Miss Temple and Helen Burns, Mary and Diana Rivers feed and nurture Jane back to life. The sisters deduce that Jane is educated from her manner of speaking, that her clothes are "fine" (289), and that her "physiognomy would be agreeable" though haggard now (289), and their brother assures her physiognomy "certainly not indicative of vulgarity or degradation" (289).

A rejuvenated Jane is welcomed into the female community at Moor House. Jane reads the books the sisters read and says of Diana and Mary, "thought fitted thought; opinion met opinion: we coincided, in short, perfectly" (298). All three are governesses, dependents. Upon discovery

that they are blood relatives – Jane's father and Rivers's mother were
siblings – Jane shares her new wealth, and the female community thrives.
At Moor House, Jane's life is literally saved, moored in safety for a while.
She learns how to dialogue with intelligent equals. She lives in a
stimulating and nurturing environment for the first time as a non-
subordinate.

The milieu is indeed encumbered by the authoritative presence of St.
John Rivers, but enough of a delightful and homey setting is worked
around him that the possibilities of a long-term peaceable coexistence
among the women can be imagined, particularly given St. John's
impending departure for mission work in India. But it is the compulsory
heterosexuality of two marriage proposals that ruins the possibility of
Jane's living in female community long term. St. John offers of marriage
and life in a foreign land, and, ultimately, Rochester's offers a second
proposal, which Jane accepts. Laura Green reminds, the "closure of
marriage obliterates the female intellectual companionship" (35).

Just as the female mentors are doubled in the novels, so too are the
male suitors/husbands. Jane has the proposals from St. John and
Rochester. Mary marries two "diseased" men, one terminally ill, the other
terminally dissipated. Jane rejects a monomaniacal man of god and accepts
a maimed man. All four are wounded male bodies. None too healthy
herself, Mary is described repeatedly, upon her return from America to
London, as "faint…from insufficient nourishment and clothes" (163). Her
face has the lines of those who "have much sensibility to suffering" (172).
Hers is a "pathetic droop of mouth" (185). In London, she is lonely, with
"few illusions left" (185). Her "work was not chosen work…[she found]
no joy in it" (186). When Jack D'Arcy, many years her senior, proposes,
he reminds Mary, "you aren't everyone's fancy" (185). She is the first
woman he has asked to marry, and underscores that the marriage would be
one last adventure, as he is terminally ill.   His is a dubious proposal, hers
a benign acceptance. He admits:

> There might, probably, be two opinions as to the advisability of your
> taking a hand with me; twenty as to my moral value as a partner. I have
> played the world off my own bat, played my own game in my own way.
> …I have loved just as many women as I have had time to, but I never
> treated one of them badly…I never loved a woman merely for the sake of
> my own gratification. (188-189)

Mary continues to be described as "weary" throughout this dubious
proposal scene. When she finally speaks, she acknowledges she is
reminded of the bowmaker and her warning to wait. D'Arcy tells her "if

you were not handicapped by your need of loving you might be a glorious adventuress; as it is you never will. You have a great capacity for love going to waste in you; why not turn a little of it over on me?" (190). Mary answers this (insulting) marriage proposal with: "Very well. I don't mind" (190).[24] Egerton strips the scene of the romance commonly attendant to proposal scenes. Mary's agency seems reduced to ennui.

Beyond this proposal scene, Egerton devotes no narrative space to Mary's first marriage, save for a few recollections at a later point. D'Arcy dies within two years, and within this time, Mary feels both "secure and insecure at the same time" (206) with D'Arcy. She puts on a kind of "armour," is "other than she really was, for the first time in her life" (204). D'Arcy is a "bully" (204) who dresses her in "furs and jewelry" (211) and gives her a "cable bracelet" on their wedding (204). When he dies, he leaves her but little money, the rest going to his two illegitimate children (250). D'Arcy embodies a patriarchy that is marked not so much by cruelty as by narcissistic opportunism.

Mary's second marriage is to Cecil Marriott, a weak, obstinate man who "disarmed women when he smiled" (197) and "simulated affection" to cajole women (216), honing this to a "fine art" (216). He reminds Mary of a "schoolboy" (208), as do most men in the novel.[25] Mary's body continues to be described as "haggard and hollow" (200). She is depressed, "numbing , baleful" (201), feels like an "automaton" (203). Mary acknowledges she "drifted" (219) into this second marriage, despite the "gulf" (215) between her and Cecil.[26] She admits she must have been asleep, "numbed" (216), but she "felt as if she were dead anyway" (217), and how else was she to "satisfy her craving for love" (216) if not this move to marry. In the days leading up to the wedding, Mary weeps and prepares her finances as if in anticipation of dying.

Mary assesses Cecil more clearly during their marriage, though her first reading of him is not debunked. His is a "cotton-wool sensibility" (263) and a "poverty" of nature (263). The marriage is a "disillusion at every stage" (271). Cecil is a gambler and drunk, a medical doctor who eschews his responsibilities, leaving them to Mary. This comes to a pitch when Mary tends to a sick woman one inclement night, and falls ill, giving premature birth to a daughter who lives but three days. [27] Mary bemoans the "tragic inevitability" (231) of her life and realizes "how evil a thing a marriage could be" (234). Mary sinks into a "calm acceptance of the facts of life in all their crudeness" (271) just before her dissipated and adulterous husband is kicked to death by a horse in a drunken-driving accident.

The reader has to wonder at Mary's susceptibility to the patriarchy embodied in her two diseased husbands. Were the lessons of the dead Septima and the esthetic bowmaker missed on Mary? Was her need for love so urgent, and her stamina so weakened, as Egerton repeatedly tells us, that she settles? While this remains nebulous in the text, what becomes evident in the narrative is that another marriage is not in the cards for Mary.

Famously, Jane Eyre's is a different relationship to marriage. Rochester arrives on the scene about a quarter of the way through the novel, at a point where Jane has done battle with embodied patriarchy that plays out as violent and narcissistic. Though he comes upon the scene with a "rude noise" and "din" (95), immediately falling off of his horse at Jane's feet, Rochester blusters that his body is unhurt, though he has a damaged ankle and must lean on Jane to get up. Further, he must ask her to hand him his whip that had fallen with him. The scene, set in nature, outside of Rochester's patriarchal mansion, prefigures the novel's final scene, set in nature as well, where Rochester no longer wields a whip and must lean on Jane, yet again.

Jane describes Rochester's body as having "great, dark eyes," "granite-hewn features" (111), and an "unusual breadth of chest, disproportionate almost to his length of limb" (111). He is an outsized man with an outsized ego who tests Jane's limits. Rochester's methods of obtaining Jane for his own are deceptive and inappropriate. Because he wields patriarchal power, he can legally imprison his wife's body; can boast about his sex experience; can misrepresent himself as a gypsy; and can cover up the stabbing and biting of Bertha's brother Mason. So full of himself is Rochester that he would have two wives, putting himself above the law and risking Jane's integrity and reputation.

Jane's experience of embodied patriarchy in husband figures prefigures Mary's experience precisely. Rochester tells her: "I will make the world acknowledge you a beauty too…I will attire my Jane in satin and lace, and she shall have roses in her hair" (221). Jane's response echoes Mary's later thoughts: "Then you won't know me, sir" (221) and "I never can bear being dressed like a doll by Mr. Rochester" (229). Rochester: "I shall waft you away at once to …French vineyards and Italian plains" (221). D'Arcy makes all of these promises to Mary. It should be noted that Rochester falls victim to a father and brother who tricked him in to marrying the beautiful and wealthy Bertha for male financial gain. This sets up a legacy of patriarchy that Rochester perpetuates in his duping of Jane. Rochester's represents patriarchy that births patriarchy as an unbroken chain.

St. John Rivers's is a different embodiment of patriarchy from Rochester's. St. John "hides a fever in his vitals" (304), his sisters tell Jane. What he shows the world, however, is utter control. Speaking with divine authority, he tells Jane:

> God and nature intended you for a missionary's wife...You shall be mine: I claim you (343)... I want a wife: the sole helpmeet I can influence sufficiently in life and retain absolutely till death. (346)

When Jane resists – but "I scorn your idea of love" (348) -- St. John threatens:

> Refuse to be my wife, and you limit yourself for ever to a track of selfish ease and barren obscurity. Tremble lest in that case you should be numbered with those who have denied the faith, and are worse than infidels! (348)

Jane "read well" his silence and "despotic manner" and "inflexible judgment" as colonizing language (349), the sort proffered by Brocklehurst, another Christian patriarch. Jane has developed the authority by now to tell him, "keep to common sense, St. John: you are verging on nonsense" (352). And later assesses him as

> a great man [who] forgets, pitilessly, the feelings and claims of little people, in pursuing his own large views. It is better, therefore, for the insignificant to keep out of his way; lest, in his progress, he should trample them down. (354)

This notion of keeping out of the way of patriarchy is pivotal. The fervor of patriarchal entitlement embodied in Rochester and St. John is not easily resisted, such is its efficacy. Learning to avoid its snare is a first step toward disempowering it.

St. John bullies with scripture repeatedly, using such cliched phrases as "lake which burneth with fire and brimstone" (355). One gentle moment against a backdrop of tyrannical claims, however, woos Jane. So enamored is she of St. John in a kinder moment, that she nearly succumbs to his proposal. "Oh, that gentleness! How far more potent is it than force!" Fortunately, one male claim on Jane is interrupted by a stronger male claim.

Jane heeds Rochester's uncanny call, makes her way back to Thornfield and then to Ferndean, and finds him reduced, symbolically castrated and thus less stridently patriarchal:

his form was of the same strong and stalwart contour as ever: his port was still erect, his hair was still raven-black; nor were his features altered or sunk, not in one year's space, by any sorrow, could his athletic strength be quelled, or his vigorous prime blighted. But in his countenance I saw a change: that looked desperate and brooding – that reminded me of some wronged and fettered wild beast or bird. (367)

Rochester, too, is gentler, tamed. Jane witnessed "the subjugation of that vigorous spirit to a corporeal infirmity" (374). Still, Rochester's is not a total transformation. "I must have you," he tells Jane. "My very soul demands you: it will be satisfied: or it will take deadly vengeance on its frame" (371), words that reproduce those of St. John. Still, Jane loves Rochester better now, she maintains, when she "can really be useful" (379) – than she could in his "state of proud independence" (379).

Jane has, indeed, learned to read books and bodies. She refuses to be bullied by males; she refuses to be dressed up by males[28]; and she enters marriage only after her partner is humbled, after she has discerned the potency of gentleness. Brontë demonstrates that a marriage of "equals" can succeed. Where Brontë concludes Jane's growth to maturity in companionate, heterosexual marriage, Egerton writes Mary Desmond beyond this conclusion.

In the later years of her life, with both husbands dead, Mary begins to read women and women's texts and, particularly, the embodied feminism of "John Morton."[29] "John Morton" is the penname of the female character who gives most explicit voice to George Egerton's ambivalent ideas about the New Woman in relation to love. Egerton reserves her introduction of Morton for the penultimate chapter. Mary is astonished at this "bit of a thistle-down...wonderful little creature" (301) who writes books for women and goes by a man's name and has a reputation for making either "stanch friends or bitter enemies" (301). Morton has a voice that is soft but with an enunciation that is "crisp and clear" (301). She looks "probingly" (301) into Mary's eyes and recognizes therein a tenderness and quiet. She reads Mary clearly, as Egerton intends her to be read by an experienced critical reader. There is a mutuality in the dialogue between Mary and Morton that constitutes a convergence of the theoretical and the experiential. Morton introduces her theories about women; Mary shares her experience as a woman. It is in the subsequent chapter, however, that Egerton creates an explicitly dialogic setting in which Morton's theory and Mary's experience reading books and bodies converge as polemic.

Where once fictional/mythological illusions bolstered the child Mary for entry into the world, such illusions are now dis-illusions. Marriage has wearied Mary. She admits she is giving up tilting "at all the wind mills," fighting "the dragons," and seizing "the golden apples locked in the Ogre's casket" (303). The irresponsible behavior of the men in her life has left her enervated, and fragmented, yet Mary needs to give love. Now, she tells Morton, she sits and gives bits of herself to those who want them. Morton invites Mary out of her domestic "corner" and into a public space with other women. Plot parallels character development here. As Mary externalizes her thinking, she moves outside of her home.

Discursive public spaces are common to New Woman novels. The function of the space is to allow an explicit voicing of ideas, usually on the topic of women or gender. In the final part of *The Wheel of God*, Mary is present in this public space and privy to the dialogue going on there, but she is not an active participant. Mary functions as a critical reader, taking in the dialogue between John Morton and several other women attending a lecture. Egerton creates a forum for the nuanced interchange of dialogue about women and love in a lecture for women given at the Sapper's Club.[30] Mary Desmond's presence at the lecture constitutes a reading of other ideological perspectives on women, perspectives that by and large affirm her own evolving thinking and reading of female bodies.

Morton, who serves as what Bakhtin would call an ideologue, is the main speaker in this scene. Hers is a relatively minor role in the plotting of the novel, but her significance as a character who voices feminist theory is profound. A Bakhtinian reading of this lecture scene is particularly illuminating in that John Morton encapsulates what could be read as a dialogue among Egerton and the famous foremothers (and father) Mary Wollstonecraft, Margaret Fuller, and John Stuart Mill.[31] Within the ideas represented by Morton can be found clear echoes of these three thinkers as well as the ambivalent glosses on these ideas that so marks George Egerton's uneasy relationship to feminism. Essentially, John Morton represents the synthesized ideas of these great minds. Morton, known as a writer of "advanced" books (309), tells her audience that the

> most striking feature in our time is the gulf between man and woman; for either she is a doll he must dress and humour, or an opponent clamouring for suffrage, and canvassing for votes in the lobby. (306)

Morton frames female yearning for love as woman's primary disability, echoing Fuller most closely when Fuller says, "It is a vulgar error that love, *a* love to woman is her whole existence" (117). What aligns Egerton's John Morton with her feminist forbears is their mutual understanding that the problem of gender inequity is not the fault of any one person or sex. Rather, it is systemic. Their critiques, then, are aimed at the authoritative discourses that uphold patriarchy and the institutions that enable them to continue in power. The socio-cultural backdrop against which men and women enter romantic relationships or marriage, from the time of Wollstonecraft to that of Egerton, is flawed. The thing called for by all of these intellectuals is what Fuller calls "genuine marriage… (the mutual choice of souls inducing a permanent union)" (91). She maintains, at mid-century, that

> we are now in a transition state, and but few steps have yet been taken, [these thwarted] …by the haste, the ignorance, or the impurity of men…man assumes a high principle to which he is not yet ripened. (Fuller 91)

Indeed, Fuller continues, "The man is not born for the woman, only the woman for the man…Men cannot understand the hearts of women" (105).[32] Toward the very end of the novel, Mary Desmond recalls earlier words of John Morton, almost verbatim Fuller: "' the men we women of to-day need, or who need us, are not of our time – it lies in the mothers to rear them for the women who follow us'" (321).[33] Change is required in law and culture and institutions. The authoritative discourses of The Woman/Marriage Question need an overhaul, as all of these feminist authors have been arguing. Revision of law must be taught, says Fuller, "by one who speaks with authority, not in anger or haste" (49). George Egerton represents her versions of women who do make such an attempt, including the grown-up Mary Desmond.

What is underscored here is a shared moment of understanding, woman to woman. Indeed, the dialogue in this scene has been heavy, but such dialogue does not turn to debate such that there are winners and losers. Mary's sentiments sum up the scene as representative of the significance of female dialogue: "'It does you good to see what other women are doing now and then; clears off the cobwebs, helps you to see the possibilities in your own corner'" (310). Mary's move from domestic to public space allows her to read her post-marital circumstances with clarity.

The dialogic interaction between women marks the final turn in the plot of Egerton's novel and Mary Desmond's development as a reader of bodies and books. Egerton, again, turns to the challenges offered by Fuller and takes her up on them. "Men," says Fuller, "as at present instructed, will not help this work [of creating egalitarian/companionate marriage], because they also are under the slavery of habit" (78). Women, then, must stop asking them for help and

> retire within themselves, and explore the groundwork of life till they find
> their peculiar secret. Then, when they come forth again, renovated and
> baptized, they will know how to turn all dross to gold. (Fuller 79)

Fuller could be speaking the mantra of New Woman fiction here: explore
and expand the discourse of marriage by exploring and expanding, first,
internally persuasive discourse and then entering dialogue with
authoritative discourses. Woman, then, must retire before coming forth
again. That is, she must refuse vexatious marriage in favor of a working
dialogic community. "At present," then, Fuller concludes, "women are the
best helpers of one another" (114). The rich tableau Egerton offers as
conclusion to Mary Desmond's story supports this belief -- female
community is the next best thing to companionate marriage.

What may be the most important note struck by Egerton regarding
Mary's reading is her framing of that heft of reading with female authors,
Charlotte Brontë on the front end and John Morton on the back. Mary
begins in dialogue with *Jane Eyre* and ends in dialogue with John Morton
and friends. Brontë is a writer Mary Desmond reads in *The Wheel of God*;
John Morton is a female journalist she meets and befriends and "reads"
toward the end of the novel. That is, before we know Mary's name, we
know that the "little child" (3) has been reading *Jane Eyre*, has an
affective response to the book, is, indeed, "a-quiver from the strangeness
of it," and is already engaged in dialogue with herself about the literary
theme of love.

> What was this love of which all the poets sang; that made men set out on
> ventures bold; and women sit and weep at lonely casements; that ran life a
> magic golden thread through every tale of romance and chivalry? (3)

Egerton sets up her frame of female texts by creating a parallel response,
even using identical words, to Mary's meeting of John Morton toward the
end of the novel. Mary is "quite stirred out of the apathy that had been
stealing over her in the last years" (306) after meeting the writer. She is
alive again and sees "quivering human interest everywhere" (315). If men
in her life experience have wrought enervation, women have brought
stimulation.

In her own novel, Egerton refracts the final setting of *Jane Eyre* at
Ferndean by implementing concave symbols of the female body where
Brontë's are assuredly male. Jane comes to Rochester's country house, as
Mary Desmond comes to the cottages, just ere dark. Both women are
going deep into nature for their final phase of life, Jane to enter a marriage
with Rochester, Mary to enter a female community. The sexual symbols of
the contrasting scenes complement these alternative endings.

Jane Eyre comes to Ferndean on an evening marked by images that are phallic and wild. A cold gale and penetrating rain (366) are falling as she passes through "iron gates between granite pillars" (366) to enter the property. Once inside, she encounters more foliage and no clear path. Proceeding, she finally comes to a railing from which she can rest and observe and read the house. What Jane sees is in marked opposition to what Mary sees. Ferndean is marked by "dense, summer foliage" (366), and Jane enters "a portal, fastened only by a latch" (367). "Can there be life here?" Jane asks of the desolation. Decaying walls, no flowers, no garden-beds, yet Brontë draws Jane to Ferndean and to Rochester with the tripled cry of longing: "Jane! Jane! Jane!" that whispered in the wind, ostensibly from a heart-weary Rochester (381).

In *The Wheel of God*, Egerton echoes this cry, "'Mary, Mary, Mary!'" (322), and she underscores Mary's sense of the animated, "vitally quiet, not dead" (320) wood she enters, a wood alive with small-animal scurrying. Both cries come from a place of "eager seeking" (Egerton 322); Rochester seeks Jane; the women in the cottages seek Mary. But in Mary's case, the female symbols welcome Mary not in neediness, but rather in openness. Mary "gazes down to the valley" (320) with its promise of life to come. In this moment, she grasps a "kernel of her being in the palm of her hand." The valley seems to stretch to a plain filled with "myriads of women" (321), and the "slender, crescent moon cut a scoop out of the sky" (321). When the "opened door of the cottage" casts a "golden bar" (321) of light onto ground, Mary's life has come full circle. Where she began with great "iron bars [that] lined the high, narrow windows" and made her think of "grim tales of dungeons" and of the "Inquisition" (3). The striking contrast between the final tableau of the feminized cottages and the rich, iron-barred nursery of the novel's opening, marks a resolution of Mary's "questioning childhood, ardent girlhood, womanhood with its disillusions" with the realization for Mary that she is stepping, at last, "into the inheritance of her self" (321). The "path was free," Egerton tells us, "for the people had risen, demolished his barriers, and established their right of way" (319). Desmond determines, amidst this community: "we often think the world is out of gear when, really, we only need to apply the tuning-fork to our own souls to find 'the hole in the ballad'" (311).

"Reader, I married him" (382) famously rounds out Brontë's novel. Her "ever more absolutely bone of his bone and flesh of his flesh" (384) suggests the troublesome concept of coverture, yet, Jane is taken with the idea of "rehumanis[ing]" Rochester (371). While Brontë represents Jane as fulfilled in marriage and motherhood, she cannot be said to be fully complicit with nineteenth-century dominant culture's view of these institutions. Laura Green makes the point that Jane's

> emphasis on 'perfect concord' has a more chilling than reassuring effect, suggesting as it does that conflict can be avoided only by absolute assimilation, as though the ideal marriage in fact embodies only one identity, whose gender remains obscure. (43)

As is evidenced by Brontë and others who wrote about intellectual women, Victorian women writers created male characters for their intellectual heroines with much difficulty. One strategy they struck was rendering bodies of male companions blind or wounded or ill. This is a pattern adopted by New Woman novelists. This notion of re-humanizing a man goes along with John Morton's notion that "' the men we women of to-day need, or who need us, are not of our time – it lies in the mothers to rear them for the women who follow us'" (321). As the men in Egerton's novel, according to John Morton, need to be trained up, so, too, the men in Brontë's novel need first be broken down then re-trained, re-"mothered" in order to be worthy of the heroines each creates. [34]

The Wheel of God is a dialogic text that resists "finalizing frame of reality" (Bakhtin, *Problems* 284). The final tableau Egerton creates to finish off her novel is rich. She is not unique in fashioning an all-female community for her heroine; Chomdeleley does so with her *Red Pottage* (1899) heroines Rachel West and Hester Gresley. And even Gissing offers up a similar living situation for his *Odd Women* (1893), but Egerton reifies the female community in contrast to heterosexual marriage. In her final tableau, there is no marriage, no motherhood. Rather, there is female connection via intellectual companionship, empathetic relation, non-hierarchy, and inviting living conditions. The novel ends with a solution that implies a waiting for a better future state, and Egerton's discussion of love in *Rosa Amorosa* offers insight in a particularly Bakhtinian way:

> Love is a religion. But you have so many forms of belief that one has to confess oneself a heretic to escape being torn to pieces in the interest of some special form of the True Faith. One has to step outside the pale of orthodoxy in order to find a quiet fane where one can commune with one's God at the altar of one's own form of worship. Love – Love is the keystone of the human bridge spanning time and eternity. (12)[35]

Just how one reads the books and bodies of love, be it "love without the lover...with none of the disturbance," as New Woman novelist Sarah Grand offers, (Grand qtd in Richardson "Allopathic" 8)[36] or love with the

New Man who has yet to come, the key to survival for the New Woman is vigilant reading.

Notes

[1] See Rachel Blau DuPlessis *Writing Beyond the Ending: Narrative Strategies of Twentieth-Century Women Writers*. Bloomington: Indiana University Press, 1985.
[2] American New Woman novelist Elizabeth Stuart Phelps quoted in Kelly 50.
[3] In her examination of New Woman writer Sarah Grand, Mangum positions reading along a spectrum of symbolic analysis. That is, women who read books are taking the first step in a larger process that will allow them to transfer their reading skills to other objects within their worlds. Just as a reader comes to have empathy for, or critical distance from a character in a book based on engagement with a character's words, thoughts, and actions as either authoritative or internally persuasive, so too, a reader will transfer such skills in taking a position regarding her own surroundings. Of course, the heroines of New Woman novels read with both resistance and identification, attempting sometimes successfully, sometimes not, to put their reading, their enhanced world views, into practice, making use of the meanings they determine make sense to them. They do, however, for the most part read alone, sharing ideas from their reading with few or with one special other. Much of what the novelists explore is the way reading informs the interiority of the heroine's psychic world.
[4] Five women's rights journals were in print during the 1850s (Anderson 186). Seminal feminist works were published including Margaret Fuller's *Woman the Nineteenth* Century (1850) and 1869 John Stuart Mill *The Subjection of Women*. Elizabeth Cady Stanton argued in 1861 that "marriage without equality became 'legalized prostitution'" (*Joyous* 188). Other feminist activist figures included Amelia Bloomer, Susan B. Anthony, Lucy Stone, Sarah and Angelina Grimke.
[5] Bonnie Anderson in *Joyous Greetings: the First International Women's Movement, 1830-1860:* At the height of the Victorian era, women dared to speak out in public about prostitution, forced marriage, the right to have sex or refuse it. They demanded that child custody be awarded to mothers instead of automatically going to fathers. They defined a new kind of marriage based on companionship and claimed the right to divorce if it failed. They saw prostitution not as a moral fault but as the direct result of an unjust economic system that forced women into only a handful of degraded and poorly paid jobs. They worried about all the victims it produced by the undervaluing of women's labor; the housewives who toiled all day but did not 'work,' the women paid wages too low to live on, the prostitutes who worked the 'fifth quarter of the day' to survive, the children who always suffered when their mothers were impoverished. (10)
[6] Laws passed during this time had significant implications for the female body. These included: Contagious Diseases Acts, Divorce and Matrimonial Causes Act

(1857), Married Woman's Property Acts (1870 and 1882), R. V. Jackson case (1891) in which husbands could no longer detain or imprison their wives.

[7] Egerton biography here

[8] Egerton's confidence in the autonomy of individual perspective becomes shadowy when she addresses the issue through the lens of gender. An essentialist slant cannot be denied in Egerton's writing She assumes an authority for women, a superiority even, that complicates a reading of her as feminist writer. She argues, for example, in *Rosa Amorosa,* that: "Outwardly woman has always seemed the more enslaved half of humanity; inwardly she has always been the more free. Whereas a man in the essence of him has always drawn either his strength or weakness from her, she has remained in her very essence unchanged, entirely uninfluenced by him, merely dependent on him for externals. For this reason ever an enigma to him! While he has been laboriously building up legal, social and moral systems, strait waistcoats for his own enslavement; woman, the eternal anarchist, has as systematically nullified his efforts, and upset his logical calculations" (177).

[9] Whose warning this is or eliminate

[10] See Mona Caird "Is Marriage a Failure?"

[11] Desmond and healthy failure to understand

[12] Bakhtin's theory of dialogue as development, as he explains it in *The Dialogic Imagination,* clarifies the struggle that I argue characterizes the New Woman heroine's evolving (feminist) consciousness. Any independent point of view on the world comes from discerning among the multiple points of view that surround every human being. The fundamental way in which such discerning is made possible is in dialogue with self and others.

[13] See Bauer's *Feminist Dialogics: Theory of a Failed Community* (1988) and *Feminism, Bakhtin, and the Dialogic (1991)* and Magnum's *Married, Middlebrow, and Militant: Sarah Grand and the New Woman Novel* (1998).

[14] New Woman novels demand that they be read another way. They neither answer nor simplify the Marriage Question; they dialogize or democratize it. That is, they complicate it by offering a dialogue that expands the discourse of the Marriage Question to include important marginalized voices and views. New Woman novels are prescient in that they call for: a de-linking of gender and domestic labor; a freely chosen motherhood; egalitarian marriage. New Woman texts are dialogic texts, and all dialogic texts, according to Bakhtin, resist finalizing frames of reality. Feminism makes the same refusals. Perhaps this is why feminist dialogic critics continue to resurrect him in order to resist, extend, critique, and challenge his thinking.

[15] Three important recent works on the figure of the woman reader in fiction serve to underscore the act of reading as it functions to educate women. Reading can be a prototypically private and interior act or an act shared with others. In either case, it is educative. For all of the New Woman heroines examined here, their primary means of education is reading. Reading was often the vehicle through which a sense of identity was achieved by fictional females, as Kate Flint maintains in *The Woman Reader 1837-1914.* In examining the *topos* of the woman reader as it

functions in cultural debate from time of Victoria's accession to World War I, Flint argues that reading "suggests the potential autonomy of [a woman reader's] mind" (4) and the inaugural step toward an "individuated subjecthood" (14). Most specifically, Flint suggests that reading is a practice that points both inward and outward – to the psychological and the socio-cultural:

The study of reading, in this as in any period, involves examining a fulcrum: the meeting place of discourses of subjectivity and socialization. Of pressing concern to those who wished to understand how the individual mind might work, and how it might develop, reading was simultaneously perceived as a prime tool in socializing; in molding a conformist, or for that matter a questioning member of society. It is therefore centrally bound in with questions of authority: authority which manifests itself in a capacity for judgment and opinion based on self-knowledge (so far as this may be possible, both in psychological terms and within the social framework of language); and authority to speak, to write, to define, to manage, and to change not just the institutions of literature, but those of society itself. (43)

In Flint's description, we can see scenes of reading in novels as sites for the examination of the Bakhtinian process of ideological becoming – reading serving, then, as the location for dialogue between heroine and authoritative discourse *and* heroine and internally-persuasive discourse. The outcome of her reading (or dialogue with books) will necessarily be, according to Bakhtin's theory, a troubling dissonance – if that reading represents authoritative discourse the heroine is unable to assimilate. It is this requisite dissonance that catalyzes the heroines' growth toward feminist thinking in the New Woman novel.

Essentially, then, as Carla Peterson posits in *The Determined Reader,* the act of reading books serves as a paradigm for understanding oneself in relation to the world. The critical ability to read texts transfers to the reading of one's own unique position in the world and one's relationship to others, given that position. Taking Peterson's theory one step further: the paradigm created by reading is offered up not just to the characters within the novels, but it is proffered for the benefit of the readers of those novels

[16] See footnote 3

[17] It is helpful to think of this reading of bodies in terms of the "gaze." Ann Kaplan explains that the gaze is not necessarily male, as ample scholarship has maintained, but that to own and activate the gaze is to be in the masculine position, or a position of authority (Kaplan 39).

[18] Such misreading, she warns, is dangerous, sometimes fatal. Citing the examples of literary heroines including Hawthorne's Zenobia (*Blithedale Romance*), Chopin's Edna Pontellier (*The Awakening*), and Wharton's Lily Bart (*The House of Mirth*), Bauer suggests that each heroine's inability to read and to assimilate her culture's ritualized, normative codes leads to her silencing by way of death.

[19] Jane Eyre's reading of Bewick's Birds has received much critical attention, thus its scant attention here.

[20] Bewick's birds ref Laura Green underscores the significance of Jane's reading: "it is Jane's salvation to be a reader rather than a Reed, drawing upon internal

imaginative and intellectual resources, rather than bending in the wind of conventional attitudes and opinions" (28).
[21] When a discourse is "authoritative," it comes to a character as something that must be obeyed, such as religious dogma, scientific truth, or even normative "truth." The "ideological becoming" of a character is begun when that character, in a moment of crisis or dissonance, realizes that there co-exist two or more meanings for the same word or idea, that some co-existing points of view on the world do not co-exist in peace, making it necessary for one to choose among them the ones that make sense to her (or are "internally persuasive"). For example, a female character might grow up among people who maintain that marriage is the only respectable choice for a woman, a holy vocation. She may not question such a perspective until she becomes conscious of another perspective on the subject that exists in the heteroglossia of her world. She may learn, for instance, that women can become artists or doctors and support themselves without ever marrying. At this point, a struggle ensues within the gap created by the uncomfortable co-existence of authoritative discourse that insists that it be obeyed and internal discourse that is critically convincing. The characters Bakhtin is interested in and the heroines I examine are those who enter this crisis of consciousness, explore the gap between what is said with authority and what is convincing to the self but unsupported by any external authority.[21] This crisis signifies the fundamental tension in the novel. The binary suggested here is, of course, overwrought. At any given time, a heroine is engaged in assimilating and assessing multiple authoritative discourses and multiple internally-persuasive discourses, and such struggles, of course, cannot all be conscious, given the nature of ideology.

What this boils down to is a character's failure to understand the "habitual ways of conceiving the world" (Bakhtin, *Dialogic* 402), an incomprehension that requires a conscious (in fiction) critical examination of the discourses surrounding one. "If we choose not to question authority," as Heikinen suggests, "we give up responsibility for any part in our own ownership and succumb to the will of the dominant culture" (122). The primary characteristic of authoritative discourse is that it will not allow itself to enter dialogue with other discourses. It sees its authority as self evident, needing only to be proclaimed, and then accepted by others. Characters for whom authoritative discourse does not make sense (make meaning) and is not critically persuasive to them, fail to read the codes of the dominant discourse(s). They mis-read. Bakhtin says they are stupid, underscoring his potentially confusing message with the insistence that "stupidity (incomprehension) in the novel is always polemical: it interacts dialogically with an intelligence (a lofty pseudo intelligence) with which it polemicizes and whose mask it tears *away*" (*Dialogic* 403). The misreading "fool," then, unmasks as fraudulent that which passes for universal or natural.

What Dale Bauer says of the female characters she studies is true of New Woman characters; they refuse

> To be silent bearers of meaning…when they exchange their sign-status for that of manipulators of signs, they do so through dialogic polemics. And, at the moment of refusal, they become threatening to the disciplinary culture

which appears naturalized. This refusal initiates the battle among voices. (*Feminist* 3)

But how does one garner a voice? Authority as a woman? What must come before the fundamental feminist behavior of misreading is reading. All of the New Woman protagonists examined here read books. All feminist critics cited here urge women to read books. Dale Bauer says, "a feminist dialogics is a paradigm which acknowledges individual acts of reading as an experience of otherness and challenges the cultural powers which often force us to contain or restrict the otherness of textual voices" (*Feminist* 5). Teresa Mangum warns that the New Woman's "failure or success depends on how well she learns to read – men's books, men's reasoning, men's means of control, and the masculine privilege that organizes the marriage plot" (90). Women must have the courage to see what they see. Feminist rebellion calls for reading another way.

[22] Cathy in Emily Brontë's *Wuthering Heights* expresses similar thoughts about heaven.

[23] Bertha Mason functions as avatar for Jane Eyre's "governed" feelings. See Gilbert and Gubar's *Madwoman in the Attic*.

[24] See Karen Tracey's *Plots and Proposals: American Women's Fiction*, 1850-90 (2000).

[25] Mary repeatedly refers to males as child like.

[26] As before, drifting into marriage

[27] Mary's loss of her only child evokes the eugenics and purity movements so significant to the writing of many New Woman novelists, including Sarah Grand. Egerton does not specifically align herself with these movements. However, the death of the child can be read as consequence of Cecil's debauched lifestyle.

[28] In significant and parallel scenes that precede the heroines living in female community, both novels show their heroines in firm resistance to their fiancés will to change their outward appearance. Mary's first husband, the terminally ill D'Arcy with whom she plans to travel during his remaining time, "rushed her off to get clothes" (203). As if an "automoton" (203), Mary feels she was, "other than she really was, for the first time in her life" (204). Jane Eyre "would rather not have [the jewels]" Rochester provides. "I will attire my Jane in Satin and lace," he says (221). "And then you won't know me, Sir," Jane retorts (221). Neither man can change the outer woman, and their inner senses of self, though shaken by men, survive intact. Brontë and Egerton expose the authoritative discourse of marriage in the action of dressing up the female, rendering her more feminine. Wives, the fiances' implicitly command, present themselves in the image of woman desired by their husbands. Jane and Mary refuse, offering their partners an alternate image of woman.

[29] The name "John Morton" alludes, arguably, to two historical figures. One was a signer of the Declaration of Independence from Pennsylvania (1724-1777). Another was the Archbishop of Canterbury (c. 1420-1500). Both men were daringly resistant to authority and its discourses. The former wrote text that led to the American Revolution, the latter wrote the history of Richard III who had him

arrested. Egerton's use of this name for most outspoken ambivalent-feminist ideas is testament to her revolutionary sentiments.

[30] A sapper is a military engineer who does demolition work; Egerton is being ironic in situating a feminist lecture here.

[31] All three writers, Fuller, Mill, and Wollstonecraft, compare the position of women in relation to men, particularly in marriage, to a form of slavery. They call for increased education and liberty for women in order for an enhanced quality of life for the species. Wollstonecraft's *A Vindication of the Rights of Woman* (1792) serves as a dialogue with male writers, particularly Rousseau and the Greeks, in which she counters their positions on women as "nonsense!" (25). Fuller's *Woman in the Nineteenth Century* (1845) serves as dialogue with those "sages and lawgivers ...[who] bent their whole nature to the search for truth" (6) and an offering of "a great difference of view" (8). Mill's *The Subjection of Women* (1869) engages in dialogue with those who uphold the fundamental premises upon which all "former arbitrary injustices and false logic" about women rested (xiii); the tenets which Mill counters are these: women are naturally inferior to men; men have a right to rule women and it is their duty to obey; marriage for women is not a state but a vocation that precludes life in the social and political world.

Additional writers are echoed Her insistence on women being educated echoes the words of Wollstonecraft, who says, "that a proper education; or, to speak with more precision, a well stored mind, would enable a woman to support a single life with dignity, I grant" (32). And John Morton alludes with irony to John Stuart Mill's famous *The Subjection of Women* in her joking about lecturing on men's powerlessness in the face of feminine ruffles ("The Subjection of Man to the Furbelow") (*Wheel* 309).

[32] Egerton gives an alternative, if not a model, embracing hope for the evolution of a New Man in the words of John Morton: In *Rosa Amorosa*, she says: "I could never be loyal to a king merely because he was king...I have stood in a crowd often, and tried to see if I felt any thrill at the passing of royalty, but an honest analysis always resulted in the knowledge that, given flags, music, and shouting people, the thrill that a common enthusiasm sends to every individual in a crowd, one might feel the same if the carriage were empty and royalty only an abstraction" (137-138). Egerton does not, however, rely on the evolution of a New Man as panacea. Moreover, Egerton makes plain that women should wait for their "messiah" (*Wheel* 208-209, 293) – for the New Man is not yet evolved enough to make a companionate marriage partner for the New Woman.

[33] On boat to America, Mary meets a well-bred Englishman who reads and analyzes her such that he surmises Mary should "go alone – you can" (65) unless she finds the "right man, and he would be an uncommon specimen. The rising generation is a poor thing, brute or decadent, or a cross between the two – to few whole men" (65).

[34] Egerton is, perhaps, clearest (and most indebted to Nietzsche)[34] on this point in *Rosa Amorosa*: "No woman in her heart really believes that she is angelic, much less an angel. That is only dear man's hyperbole....Man created woman – out of what, then? Out of a rib of his God – the ideal. He did more: he fashioned in

accordance with his own ideas a pair of wings for her, and she has worn them ever since to please him – but the first thing a company of women of the world do, when they are alone together, is to lay them aside with relief. (54-56)

[35] Not all New Woman novelists or New Woman activists agree on the way marriage should look, but all do agree that it is not working at the end of the late nineteenth century for women and that the problem is systemic. All certainly embrace the notion of the companionate marriage; in its varied ideal forms, it is part of New Woman history. Egerton does not reject marriage outright. She does, however, reject any infringement on the freedoms of either party in a romantic relationship. The suggestion here, as in other New Woman novels, is that successful heterosexual love within marriage is possible under certain conditions. Margaret Fuller: "The curse of the whole system is, of course, the fact of making a condition based on mutable feelings subject to immutable laws. (133-134)

[36] Recent scholarship on the New Woman novel claims that "In a way typical of New Woman novels, the story ends with the heroine's suicide" [36](re GrantAallen). Nothing could be farther from the truth when one examines New Woman novels written by *women.* To extrapolate from texts of dubious motivation by men is facile at best. Egerton's is seminal to our understanding of the authority with which female New Woman writers imbue their heroines. And Egerton is one of many. Nevertheless, her *Wheel of God* demonstrates that the female authority of the foremother (Brontë) can and does inform the evolutionary and radical writing beyond monologic and patriarchal ideologies.

CHAPTER SIX

THE PHYSICAL PRICE OF FREEDOM:
EXHAUSTED PROTAGONISTS
AND URBAN FELLOWSHIP

KELLY HULANDER

Feminist scholars of the British New Woman phenomenon explain that the concept of the New Woman was originally a discursive tool employed in print for a variety of political and social aims and a term used to describe a range of lifestyles that real women were increasingly adopting in late-century Britain[1]. Sally Ledger writes that the New Woman was "largely an urban phenomenon, a significant presence in the city landscapes of the second half of the nineteenth century" (150). Deborah Epstein Nord, illuminating the lives of three unconventional women writers living in 1880s London, states that the city offered young women "the possibility of social and economic independence" and a place in which to carry out their "revolt against the constraints of bourgeois family life"—a place, in fact, in which to define themselves anew (183). Although their lifestyle choices helped fuel the discursive blaze that was the late-century New Woman debate, Talia Schaffer reports that most of these women lived unglamorous lives, typically working as "clerks, typists, teachers, college students, journalists, or perhaps even shopgirls" and occupying "spartan flats...living primarily on bread and tea" (39). Such self-reliant women were removed from both the comforts and the established communal ties of their middle- and upper-middle-class homes; their work or studies in London often forced them to live economically and to form new circles in which to move, work, and survive.

It is representations of these social circles, especially those appearing in New Woman novels, which form my primary interest in *fin-de-siècle* discourse. The varieties of types of community or social bonds imagined in New Woman fiction have not been explored in sufficient depth, to date. If *fin-de-siècle* women novelists were rejecting the married-with-country-property ending of earlier works of nineteenth-century British fiction, including the local communities thereby provided, how and with whom did they imagine their protagonists bonding? Ann Ardis offers an excellent reading of supportive relationships between women in New Woman fiction[2], and Sally Ledger discusses the "emergent lesbian identity" represented in some of these works[3], but what of the possibilities for meaningful relationships beyond their groups of like-minded sisters? This essay begins to answer such questions by exploring and interpreting important relationships represented in four New Woman novels written by women and published between 1888 and 1900: Amy Levy's *The Romance of a Shop* (1888), Ella Hepworth Dixon's *The Story of a Modern Woman* (1894), Sarah Grand's *The Beth Book* (1897), and Gertrude Dix's *The Image Breakers* (1900).

These works all share a storyline in which their middle- or upper-middle-class female protagonists occupy rented rooms in London, working for self-support or pursuing their professional aims on a limited allowance.[4] Dixon's Mary Erle must provide for both herself and her younger brother when her father dies suddenly (their mother being already deceased). Levy's Lorimer sisters—Gertrude, Lucy, Fanny, and Phyllis—open a photography studio when they meet with the same fate. Dix sends Leslie Ardent[5] to the city to make her way as a commercial artist, while Sarah Grand's aspiring author, Beth Maclure, actually lives twice in London: once in the stylish home of upper-class friends and, more to the purpose for this essay, a second time alone in a rented attic room. In discussing contemporary reviews of Levy's novel, Linda Hunt Beckman reveals that such plotlines were familiar to late-century British readers (154-5), yet, as we shall see, the energy with which participants in public discourse debated women's independence at the *fin de siècle* suggests that the topic of middle-class woman's self-support in urban settings was still controversial.

My study of themes of community and relationship in these works has revealed three useful lenses through which this material can be viewed. The first is the concept of "fellowship," defined as both "community of interest, sentiment, or nature" and "intimate personal communion" (*Shorter OED* 940). The protagonists in these novels are all represented as women yearning for fellowship, and the relative happiness of their stories' endings correlates directly to their success in finding it. Interestingly, most of the fictional New Women discussed here ultimately find lasting fellowship with male characters—all variable representations of the New Man.

The second useful focus for issues of communion in these works is the protagonist's imagined body itself; or, more properly, her overworked and exhausted body. These urban New Women pay a high physical toll for their freedoms and their friendships; indeed, for three of the four, a period of acute exhaustion is required before they can secure the sustaining relationships that will define their ultimate fulfillment. Levy, Grand, and Dix all imagine a protagonist's body that gains its communal authority via a period of self-denial and exacting toil.

The Story of a Modern Woman also features a protagonist pushed to her physical limits by economic and social necessity; sadly, even exhaustion cannot help Dixon's Mary Erle find human fellowship. Deborah Parsons writes that "the educated working woman living in the city, and not financially supported by her family, had to subsist on the meager level of female earnings" (110); Mary's fictional body becomes a testimony to the possible costs of such subsistence. Since Dixon is writing a late-century tragedy, designed to underscore the single woman's vulnerability in a sexist culture, her New Woman's physical and emotional trials necessarily end in loneliness. Indeed, Mary Erle's ultimate isolation highlights the central role that women novelists assigned to fellowship in shaping the New Woman's happiness.

Finding the third lens helpful for understanding the aforementioned themes required me to step back in time a bit in terms of literary scholarship and theory. I found the key to opening these texts—to explaining this process of fellowship earned through an experience of extreme personal stress—in both the solo work of Carol S. Pearson on heroic archetypes and her collaborative project with Katherine Pope entitled *The Female Hero in American and British Literature*. I want to argue here that Grand, Levy, Dixon, and Dix use their novels to present the independent urban woman as an admirable, archetypal hero[6]. Especially for Grand, Dixon, and Dix, whose novels came out when public discourse teemed with vilifications of the New Woman—featuring portrayals of her as a brusque Amazon, an immoral sex-fiend, or an unsexed egghead—it was important to recast this besieged figure in heroic terms.

The negative presentations of New Womanhood in the mainstream press of the British *fin-de-siècle* have been well-documented. Angelique Richardson and Chris Willis explain that "*Punch* seized upon New Woman fiction as an easy target for parody, cashing in on the New Woman's diversity, while simultaneously seeking to reduce her to misandrous stereotypes that were either having too much or too little sex" (13). By focusing on a few rising trends in female behavior, including "smoking, rational dress, and bicycling," late-century cartoonists were able to frighten and entertain the public with images of the New Woman as "either...a bespectacled, physically degenerate weakling or as a strapping Amazon who could outwalk, outcycle, and outshoot any man" (Richardson and Willis 13). Patricia Marks reports that middle- or upper-middle-class women who worked for pay, either out of economic necessity or personal choice, were frequently targeted for criticism in the popular press; Marks gives the example of an essay entitled, "The Wild Women as Social Insurgents," published in *Nineteenth Century* by Eliza Lynn Linton (herself a journalist and novelist), in which Linton "decries the desire of women to work, which she believes, undertaken for the mischievous desire to shock, causes unemployment among the needy" (8). This proliferation of public negativity about progressive and self-reliant women cried out for an alternative model of New Womanhood; Levy, writing just before the greatest force of the anti-New Woman explosion was felt, and Grand, Dixon, and Dix, entering the full heat of this discursive war, all offered heroic protagonists as their positive fictional alternatives.

In *The Female Hero in British and American Literature*, Pearson and Pope study literary representations of the female hero from the eighteenth through the mid-twentieth centuries. In terms of texts from the British *fin-de-siècle*, *The Female Hero* provides detailed readings of Thomas Hardy's *Tess of the D'Urbevilles* and George Gissing's *The Odd Women*. Characterizing Hardy's novel as a work that "educates the reader about the deleterious effects of sex-role definitions on women's lives," Pearson and Pope argue that Hardy portrays Tess as "a complete woman, who is both sexual and spiritual, experienced and virtuous," thereby challenging stereotypical roles for women, while "mak[ing] it clear that she need not have died if societal institutions and myths about female virtue had been more reasonable" (165). They find in Gissing's novel another critique of gender-role failures, but see in *The Odd Women* a specific statement on the paucity of late-century New Men: Gissing's most progressive female character, Rhoda Nunn, "remains single because there is no man in her world who is her equal in passion, intellect, character, or courage" (153).

In this essay, I build on the work done by Pearson and Pope in three ways: first, by exploring novels by women writers whose works were neither easily available nor widely known in the 1980s; second, by showing how three of these novels set themselves apart from works like *Tess* and *The Odd Women* by offering hopeful models for positive heterosexual relationships at the *fin de siècle*; and, finally, by exploring more closely than Pearson and Pope the fictional representations of the female hero's body. Examining these images of heroic corporeality, I find that even authors who wished to imagine "happy endings" for their New Woman protagonists felt the need to temper their optimism by including physical suffering in their portrayals of female heroism.

Pearson and Pope describe the heroic quest as a "journey," the first stage of which "is the flight, escape, or expulsion from the garden or cage" that has kept the would-be hero from developing her independence and sense of self (69). Threatened by "destruction or imprisonment" in traditional gender roles, the hero must "[affirm] her independence and responsibility for her own life" (Pearson and Pope 16, 79, 82). In the novels in question here, successful flight from the garden or cage involves an element of physical testing of the protagonist. Hard work and bodily fatigue are part of a process of detoxifying and separating the New Woman from her old, bourgeois ties and lifestyle.

Grand is quite direct in stating that Beth needs a thorough cleansing from the toxic effects of her unhappy marriage to an unprincipled man:

> [Beth] was therefore as glad to leave Maclure as he was to get rid of her; and already it seemed as if with her married life a hampering weight had fallen from her, and left her free to face a promising future with nothing to fear and everything to hope. Poverty was pleasant in her big bright attic, where all was clean and neat about her. There she could live serenely and purify her mind by degrees of the garbage with which Dan's habitual conversation had polluted it. (489)

Here, Grand gives Beth the opportunity to tidy the private spaces of both her rented attic and her psyche. Although she has wealthy friends who share her progressive opinions on women's work and proper social roles, Beth must leave her past entirely behind and "drop altogether out of her own world" in order to face the trials that will prepare her for emotional and professional fulfillment (494).

Levy uses the necessities of relocating and establishing their photographic business to cleanse the Lorimer girls of the detritus of their suburban social pasts. Gertrude and her well-heeled, loyal friend, Connie Devonshire, spend "many weary days…pac[ing] the town from end to end" in search of a rental situation that will offer the orphaned girls a combination of living and studio space. Once a suitable spot is found, Levy describes a "period of absorbing and unremitting toil" in which the sisters, with the help of Conny and her brother Fred, try to save money by doing "everything, within the limits of possibility, themselves" to make the rented rooms habitable and viable for their business (77). Like Beth, the Lorimers "[drop] off from the old set, from the people with whom their intercourse had been a mere matter of social commerce;" meanwhile, "many of their friends [draw] closer to them in the hour of need" (82).

Here, Levy employs the labor-intensive process of setting up shop as a social sifting mechanism, sorting the false friends from the true; this removal of artificial relationships will help prepare Gertrude, especially, to find lasting fellowship.

Recognizing the soul-cramping nature of dependency, Dix uses the struggle for self-support to purge from Leslie Ardent the taint of dominant relationships: both her condescending socialist mentor, Rosalind Dangerfield[7], and her bossy, conservative Aunt Julia wish to abort Leslie's quest for independence and self-discovery in London. Dix tests Leslie's physical endurance at the outset of her mission: initially failing to sell her illustrations, she quickly runs low on both energy and funds. One desperate afternoon, hoping to delay total physical breakdown, she turns to "a secluded corner" in "the island of refuge" that is the British Museum, where "grateful for so much rest and shelter...she [sinks] down exhausted, to fall asleep" (107 -8). A timely loan and accurate professional advice save Leslie from the suffocating options of becoming a governess, returning to her Aunt's country home, or joining Rosalind in a socialist commune: for Dix, the New Woman hero must outlast the fatigue of establishing an urban career if she is to control her own destiny.

Dixon, too, removes Mary from her comfortable life in fashionable society, but this removal is less a passage of purification than a fall from grace. To be sure, once having lived alone and studied art in a London school for some months, Mary is able to view her former social set from an ironic distance: at a gathering hosted by Lady Jane Ives, mother of her stylish and loving friend Alison, Mary "[sits] on one side and look[s] at the little comedy with impartial eyes," finding "Vanity Fair" a "curiously foolish" community (74). Despite her tendency to lampoon the fashionable set, Dixon still paints the loss of an aesthetically-appealing and restful existence as lamentable. When Mary is tired and discouraged in her pursuit of paid employment, she longs "to creep back, just for once" to her father's former home "in Harley Street, with its indefinable air of perfect taste and perfect comfort; to the little tea-table near the fire, with its silver kettle, its dainty china, and the hot-cakes which cook used to make so well" (84). Independence, in Dixon's tragic novel, is not worth the exchange of Harley Street comfort for the "grimy back-yard" and "small iron bed with starved-looking pillows" of the Bulstrode Street rental that Mary occupies after her father's death (85).

Once free of the chains binding her to traditional roles and repressive (if posh) environments, the fictional New Woman can move on to the second phase of her heroic journey, which Pearson and Pope describe as a needed "fall from innocence into experience," in which the hero learns that she can use her own skills and intelligence to overcome difficulties and meet her goals (68). Through this process, the protagonist seeking self-reliance will come to understand that "the qualities she believed were masculine and therefore looked for outside herself are also hers" (Pearson and Pope 68). In our four New Woman novels, the major battles fought are those for financial security, professional success, and urban fellowship. Unfortunately, since, in the eyes of mainstream society, the female protagonists in these works possess the wrong sorts of bodies (i.e., women's) to wage such battles, they must perform especially great feats of physical endurance before succeeding. In order to make the heroic New Woman palatable to a reading public trained to associate womanhood with domesticity and self-sacrifice, these portrayals of the female protagonist must blend the warrior archetype with that of the martyr.

In *The Hero Within*, Pearson identifies six archetypal roles that people often embody in the course of their lives, the goal being to blend useful elements of several archetypes in order to become truly heroic or self-actualized. The warrior archetype, which Pearson argues has been misidentified as the true hero in U.S. culture, represents the individual's ability to stand up for herself, to make life-affirming decisions, and to establish and protect her boundaries (74 – 5). Unfortunately, the warrior-hero is typically cast as a white male in a racist and patriarchal society, so successful warrior-hood is often a fraught process for "women, minority men, and the working class" (Pearson 75). If Pearson saw trouble ahead for women warriors in 1989, imagine the barriers blocking a would-be New Woman hero in 1894. On the other hand, since self-sacrifice was an acceptable behavior for Victorian women—who, as Walter Houghton reports, were expected to stay home and devote themselves to protecting their families from "the amoral and irreligious drift of modern industrial society" (348)—our four New Woman authors tempered each of their warrior-heroes with a stiff dose of the martyr archetype.

In describing the archetypal martyr, Pearson is careful to distinguish between "pseudo-martyrdom," which involves "sacrificing parts of [the self] in an effort to get validation" from some external source (101), and "transformative sacrifice," which is "given freely as an expression of genuine love and care" (103). At the level of literary production, our New Woman authors, whether consciously or not, may have been martyring their protagonists for some degree of public approval. In the internal logic of their respective storylines, though, Beth Maclure, Gertrude Lorimer, and Leslie Ardent, at least, make their sacrifices willingly in the service of their loved ones. As Pearson and Pope explain, "community" is the natural "reward that the hero…[earns] by successfully completing some aspect of the journey" (247); the communal rewards they reap as a result of their self-sacrifices confirms these characters' martyr-heroics as positive and transformative acts.

As stated above, the protagonists discussed here are mixtures of warrior- and martyr-heroes. When appearing in their warrior states, New Woman protagonists enter boldly into London life and enjoy the fruits of their labors. The experience of living independently in London is also shown to heighten each protagonist's general connection to and awareness of her body; it is as if our four authors insist that earning one's keep is equivalent with experiencing embodiment. When feeling their strength as warrior-heroes, New Woman characters find in this heightened physical awareness opportunities to discover new physical pleasures. Enjoying the early effects of her purification, Beth Maclure feels her body's abilities and appetites in positive ways:

> Beth fetched up the water overnight for her bath in the morning, and made coffee for her breakfast on the little oil-stove. She lived principally on bread and butter, eggs, sardines, salad, and slices of various meats bought at a cook-shop and carried home in a paper. Sometimes, when she felt she could afford it, she had a hot meal at an eating-house for the good of her health; but she scarcely required it, for she never felt stronger in her life, and so long as she could get good coffee for her breakfast and tea for her evening meal, she missed none of the other things to which she had been accustomed. (491)

Part of a recurring critique of the excesses of fashionable life that appears in Grand's novel, this scene reveals the possible physical benefits to middle- and upper-middle-class women of a lifestyle based on self-reliance. Developing new muscle-tone through climbing stairs and hauling supplies, and enjoying the freshness of an appetite not over-indulged, Beth finds in her own body a welcome companion.

Another source of physical pleasure identified in these works is the New Woman's unchaperoned encounter with London itself. Sally Ledger reports that "the New Woman in the modern city tended to be mobile and self-confident in public places" (154). On her solitary walks around the city, taken as breaks from her writing sessions, Grand's Beth "learn[s] to appreciate the wonder and beauty of the most wonderful and beautiful city every seen…her eyes [grow] deep from long looking and earnest meditation upon it" (493). Similarly, Levy's Gertrude "contemplate[s] the familiar London pageant with an interest that ha[s] something of passion in it;" she loves living "where the pulses of the great city could be felt distinctly as they beat and throbbed" (80). Gertrude also feels "a secret, childish love for the gas-lit street, for the sight of the hurrying people, the lamps, the hansom cabs, flickering in and out the yellow haze, like so many fire-flies" (105). As Deborah Epstein Nord argues, "*The Romance of a Shop* succeeds at conveying how difficult and yet how exhilarating it was to be a woman alone in London in the 1880s" (201); Deborah Parsons also explains that "London pervades Levy's writings, as a source of inspiration and subject, but also as a place of support and nurture that she is at home within" (88). Far from the all-important country walks so loved by Jane Austen's heroes, these late-century protagonists stretch their urban muscles and find joy in London scenes. Grand and Levy especially link the New Woman's authority to traverse and enjoy the city as an expression of her physical and mental health.

As vital settings for city adventures, modes of public transport, especially omnibuses, become sites of either intense pleasure or pain for New Woman protagonists[8]. Deborah Parsons describes the omnibus as the "supreme symbol of commercial London...frequently employed by women writers as an expression of their entry into once restricted public spaces;" she states that it gave women "a means of traversing the city that passes through different social and class-defined spaces, independence amidst a crowd, and shelter from both the elements and the appropriating glances of others" (97). Indeed, as symbols of the independent woman's increasing freedom to move about the city, public transportation becomes a litmus test for the female warrior-hero's relative success in acclimating to city life. In her early, vigorous condition as a solitary renter, Beth finds

> in the new view of London and of London life from the top of omnibuses more of the unexpected, of delight, of beauty for the eyes and of matter for the mind, of humour, pathos, poetry, of tragedy and comedy, suggestive glimpses caught in passing and vividly recollected, than she could have conceived possible when she rolled along with society on carriage cushions, soothed by the stultifying ease into temporary sensuous apathy. (Grand 495)

Charmed and inspired by her new method of travel, Beth doesn't miss her former, comfier conveyances; this contentment with her lot is a positive sign of her urban adaptability. Similarly, Gertrude's love of London is reflected in the scene which finds her "careering up the street on the summit of a tall, green omnibus, her hair blowing gaily in the breeze" (Levy 99).

For Dixon's ill-fated Mary, unfortunately, the omnibus is only "stuffy" and "jolting," even when the intoxicating effect of having earned her first wages renders her "conscious of neither hunger, fatigue, nor rattling stones" (108). Here, Mary's dislike of public transport is just one symptom of her general disharmony with her independent existence. Although Sally

Ledger states that "Mary's physical possession of the city is quite confident" (158), it brings her no happiness. Like Mary Erle, Dix's Rosalind Dangerfield hates taking public transportation; "instinctively dislik[ing]" omnibuses, where people "jostled and jarred upon her nerves," she is equally disdainful of the "dirty, ill-smelling" tram cars filled with workers headed home (283, 373). Here, Rosalind's revulsion at traveling with the common people highlights her hypocrisy as an idealistic socialist: she wants to save abstract multitudes of workers from their oppression, but she shrinks from contact with actual working people and feels an insurmountable "barrier" between herself and her fellow factory workers (372). Rosalind's inability to adapt cheerfully to her urban surroundings is just one sign that her storyline in Dix's novel will end badly, while Leslie Ardent—who learns to move comfortably about the city—will eventually find happiness.

Despite experiencing increased mobility and powerful—if fleeting—flashes of pleasure, each of our fictional New Women must ultimately test her tolerance for physical suffering if she is to secure lasting fellowship (or, in Mary's case, to lose all hope of securing it). Carefully contrasting their female heroes with the strapping, Amazon-like parodies of New Women in the popular press, these novelists soften their protagonists while simultaneously demonstrating their capacities for dedication and hard work by giving them attributes of the martyr archetype. Of course, female martyrdom in the novel is by no means an invention of progressive *fin de siècle* fiction; indeed, by adopting a familiar image of self-sacrifice on the part of the female protagonist, our New Woman writers seek to gain readers' acceptance of the more progressive and potentially controversial lifestyle choices of their heroes.

In nineteenth-century novels with a more conservative ethos than the New Woman texts examined here, physical exhaustion and self-sacrifice tend to be used to improve the character of the female hero and to prepare her for marriage with a great man. Margaret Hale in Elizabeth Gaskell's *North and South* (1855), for example, develops an independent conscience and a thirst to "speak and act the truth forevermore" only after she has exhausted herself tending to the needs of others. After nearly prostrating herself with a series of acts of martyr-heroism—including nursing, then burying, her mother; sneaking her "wanted" brother safely out of England; comforting the dying and bereaved among her working-class friends; and, finally, burying her father—Margaret at last pauses to grieve her own "fatal year, and all the woes it…[has] brought to her" (401) and makes her ultimate resolution to mend past failings by embracing an ethos of personal integrity. Soon after this completion of her adult conscience,

Margaret is united with Mr. Thornton, the captain of industry whose love and wealth she is now prepared to accept. Similarly, in an interesting take on fictional New Womanhood, the idealistic Marcella Boyce of Mary Augusta Ward's *Marcella* (1894) also tests her physical and emotional endurance through service to others: she first helps a working-class woman survive the poaching trial and subsequent execution of her husband; then completes a demanding year of practical nurse's training in a London hospital; and finally works—sometimes at great physical peril— as a nurse in one of London's most impoverished districts. These experiences with actual poverty and personal self-sacrifice are part of a process through which Marcella comes to value the love and tolerate the world-view of Aldous Raeburn, the socially-aware but essentially conservative Lord whom she finally marries. Like Gaskell, Ward uses the plotline of sustained exertion and self-sacrifice on the part of the female hero to prepare her protagonist for life as the wife of a wealthy and powerful man.

For authors preferring to marry the female hero to a progressive New Man, rather than an industrial giant or a country peer, martyr-heroics are still a useful fictional strategy. Taking familiar images of women suffering and making personal sacrifices but applying them toward new ends, authors like Levy, Dix, Dixon, and Grand strive both to chronicle the actual difficulties of carving out an independent existence in late-century London and to make the unconventional lives of their urban heroes acceptable to their reading public. Although potentially disappointing to later generations of feminist scholars, giving their female heroes a streak of martyrdom is a smart discursive tactic in these authors' battle to gain public approval of the New Woman. Recognizing that freedoms come at a cost, our New Woman authors ask their protagonists to pay for the authority to live and love as they choose in the currency of physical and emotional suffering.

Beth Maclure, who forms a deep connection with her rental housemate, the painter Arthur Brock, sacrifices her health for his while nursing him through rheumatic fever. In a telling parallel, Beth's body deteriorates as their friendship grows. That they are entering into a truly "intimate personal communion" is made clear when Beth accidentally discovers Arthur's illness; she chides him for not calling to her for help, saying, "We are all of the same family here, you know...the great human family...you had only to say 'Sister!' and I should have come" (497). When Arthur gazes gratefully at her in response, Grand cements the dignity and respect of their attachment, writing that "each had seen in the other's face at the same time something there is no human utterance to describe, and, recognising it, had reverently held their peace" (497). Unfortunately, the toll on Beth of this important bond will be high: she will spend "many weeks...beside the sick man's bed," "snatching" only "brief intervals of rest" and "concealing her weariness" to avoid worrying him (499). As Kimberly Reynolds and Nicola Humble state, "the levels of repression and self-denial [Beth] forces on herself are enormously damaging" to her health, but "they are also presented as formative," for it is through this self-sacrifice that her "personality is completed" (97). In learning to give freely to another, Beth, as martyr-hero, demonstrates her mature selfhood and readiness for fellowship. Although her self-sacrifice on behalf of a man might be read as a conservative gesture, Beth is not a throwback to forced domesticity because she makes an independent choice to help Arthur Brock, and she does so at least in part because he is a model for the New Man. She enters freely into her time of martyrdom, not playing out one of the socially-prescribed roles of sister, mother, daughter, or wife, but acting in her self-imposed role as his friend and equal.

Gertrude Lorimer also suffers greatly to earn the kinds of fulfilling relationships she desires; unlike Beth, however, she carries the burden of her entire family on her small frame. Seeking her ideal of "a society not of class, caste, or family—but of picked individuals," Gertrude, as part warrior-hero, is willing to challenge accepted definitions of propriety in her search for urban fellowship (115). Defending to her aunt their mutually-sustaining (but completely unchaperoned) friendship with Frank Jermyn, their artist-neighbor, Gertrude asserts that

> we have taken life up from a different standpoint, begun it on different bases. We are poor people, and we are learning to find out the pleasures of the poor, to approach happiness from another side. We have none of the conventional social opportunities for instance, but are we therefore to sacrifice all the conventional social enjoyment? You say that we 'follow Mr. Jermyn to his studio;' we have our living to earn, no less than our lives to live, and in neither case can we afford to be the slaves of custom. Our friends must trust us or leave us; must rely on our self-respect and our judgment. Convention apart, are not judgment and self-respect what we most of us do rely on in our relations with people, under any circumstances whatever? (101)

Levy uses this speech to educate her middle-class readers on the necessity of reassessing social traditions in the face of urban New Womanhood. Lack of funds for making the usual social rounds, "the salt of healthy objective interests" shared with New Men (99), and the internal clamoring for human fellowship all require a rethinking of social taboos on behalf of London's independent youth. The fact that Gertrude's speech makes no impress on her aunt's thinking may indicate a skepticism on Levy's part about her readers' abilities to grasp these new circumstances, but she does reward her plucky protagonist with "contact with all sorts and conditions of men, among them, people in many ways more congenial...than the mass of their former acquaintance" and opportunities to "taste the sweets of genuine work and genuine social intercourse" (135).

Unfortunately, admission to this new circle of equals costs Gertrude's body rather dearly. When Phyllis falls ill, Gertrude "perform[s] prodigies of work without any conscious effort," as "frozen, tense, silent" she keeps the photography business going while nursing her youngest sister, "moving as if in obedience to some hidden mechanism, a creature apparently without wants, emotions, or thoughts" (175). Her exhausted state forces Lucy, returned from an out-of-town trip, to cry "what have you been doing to yourself?...Gertrude, Gertrude, what has happened to you?" (176). When Phyllis finally dies of consumption, their family friend, Lord Watergate, exclaims to Gertrude, "Miss Lorimer...you must do something to get well...you have been looking after everybody else; doing everybody's work, bearing everybody's troubles" (187). Here, Gertrude's role as the martyr-hero is obvious: the remaining Lorimers will survive this tragic loss, but only because Gertrude redeems them by her labors.

In the pattern of Beth and Gertrude, Leslie Ardent also makes significant physical sacrifices in her pursuit of lasting fellowship. Although Leslie does not, like Gertrude, enjoy a wide circle of friends in London, this is because Dix's primary concern with Leslie's storyline in *The Image Breakers* is with modeling positive sexual partnerships. To be sure, Leslie does strike up a friendly working relationship with Bertie Webb, a fellow aspirant to success in commercial art. It is Bertie who teaches Leslie the technical skills needed to get her work published; once her career is launched, he also lets her join the figure drawing sessions in his studio. Beyond that, however, Leslie's eyes are all for John Redgold, her lover. Earning his respect and affection is actually the underlying motive of her bid for independence, and she endures much in this pursuit.

Even after Leslie survives her initial poverty and eventual illness, and once both her commercial success and their sexual affair have been established, Redgold's old-fashioned ideal of love still takes a toll on her. As Sally Ledger states, "Redgold's mainstream radicalism is associated in the novel with old-fashioned gender relations" (57). When he demands that they become engaged, Leslie suffers, losing her grasp on her hard-earned warrior-hero status. Dix writes that Leslie "lost heart in her work, felt out of tune and touch with the cheerful life at Webb's studio," eventually losing her "concentration" and even "mastery over herself"

(238). Redgold backslides into Old Manhood when insisting that he support Leslie financially in marriage, a move that, for him, would mean working for a Liberal MP, thereby betraying his radical political beliefs. Seeing that their marriage would ensnare Redgold in political falsehood, Leslie clings to financial independence, selling her jewelry and scouring the city for buyers for her illustrations. Quietly starving herself as the martyr-hero, Leslie becomes physically unhealthy; Redgold, thinking she is merely sulking, is annoyed to find her "sitting listlessly" by her hearth, looking "pale" (314). Finally, in a last effort to save him from self-betrayal, Leslie breaks off their engagement and flees to her Aunt Julia's country home, dispirited and utterly exhausted.

Like Beth, Gertrude, and Leslie, Dixon's Mary Erle martyrs herself in a way that endangers her health. Having abandoned her failed art career for a more workable venture into journalism and creative writing, Mary suffers physically from her new trade: her back becomes "tired with bending over a desk" all day, and she grows "wretchedly weak," finding the "strain of writing…intense" (154). Mary's trials are exacerbated by her need to support a spoiled younger brother; hoping to get him through school and launched in society as a gentleman, she pushes herself mercilessly to provide him with fine clothes and ample spending money. Since she reaps so little personal enjoyment from her heroic efforts, Mary's hardships as a martyr-hero are particularly poignant.

Interestingly, even when blending in their heroes aspects of both the warrior and the martyr, New Woman writers recognize that their novels will be vulnerable to misinterpretation. As if confronting the reading public with its own habit of misunderstanding the New Woman, three of these four authors subject their protagonists to gross misreadings at the hands of male characters. In Grand's work, Arthur misreads Beth twice; first, as Teresa Mangum explains, he wounds Beth when she wants to tell him "about her divorce proceedings," and he declines, "assum[ing] that she must be at fault" in her troubled marriage (189). Although Beth moves past this misjudgment of her, she is devastated by his second offence. Eventually, as the costs of Arthur's treatments force Beth to starve and impoverish herself, financial necessity finally drives her to a desperate act which Arthur fails to comprehend. Tested by "poverty, anxiety, and fatigue," Beth sells her gowns, jewelry, and, finally, her hair to keep him eating well while she goes hungry (504). Arthur's misreading of her haircut is his major act of sexism—he accuses her of being some kind of crazed female militant—and it drives the two of them apart. When Arthur, suddenly grown cold to Beth, leaves their cozy attic life to finish recuperating at a friend's rural home, she finally collapses in a death-like state. It is his misunderstanding of her sacrifice that ultimately prostrates her; his flash of Old Manhood acts like a poison to her already-stressed frame.

In Dix's novel, Leslie's separation from Redgold also results from his misinterpretation of her and her desires. When she initially tries to break off their engagement, wishing to affirm her independence and salvage his political ideals, he treats her with irritation and condescension, calling her concerns "nonsense" and accusing her of testing his patience "beyond endurance" (253–5). Thinking that her hesitation to marry him is selfishly motivated, and not realizing that she is starving herself for his freedom, Redgold finds Leslie's pale, tired form unattractive and starts drifting toward the prosperous niece of his Liberal MP employer.

As in the cases of Beth and Leslie, Mary's physical state is misread by the men in her life. Ignoring the fiscal motivation for her toil, Vincent Hemming, the fiancé who will abandon her to marry money, chides Mary condescendingly for appearing "fatigued" and not avoiding London's "sultry weather" by taking some trip that she cannot afford (132). Even her doctor can't comprehend the fact that her work, which is putting such a "strain on [her] nervous system," is not optional; heedless of Mary's solitary existence, he writes her a prescription for a tonic of "arsenic, iron, and strychnine," and advises that "all you young ladies" should really be "living a healthy out-of-door life, happily married, with no mental worries" (176 – 7). Unable to take the doctor's romantic advice, even as she swallows his poisonous prescription, Mary loses Vincent to his wealthy wife and continues alone in her professional struggle.

Whatever her specific storyline, the New Woman protagonist pays dearly when a male character misinterprets either her actions or her circumstances: her physical suffering increases, her authority to direct her life is undermined, and her hopes of finding lasting fellowship are jeopardized by his misunderstanding. In these examples, we see New Woman writers highlighting both the pain caused by individual men who fail to treat progressive women with respectful understanding and the destructiveness of the public's misreadings of such women in their attempts to create new lives and improved standards for heterosexual love.

As I've said, Mary Erle never does find fellowship, but the rest of our heroes' tales have happier endings. Pearson and Pope explain that "the true hero—whether male or female—moves past hierarchical ways of interacting with other people and recognizes everyone's heroic potential" (251), a trait which holds true with the fictional New Man. Before his reading error, Grand draws Arthur Brock as an excellent candidate for New Manhood: Beth admires his "uncomplaining fortitude, his gentleness, gratitude, and unselfish concern about her fatigue" (499), and she revels in her "close association with a man of the highest character and the most perfect refinement…so heroic in suffering, so unselfish, and so good" (504- 5). Indeed, Arthur proves to have feminist inclinations himself, answering her claims that cooking for him is woman's work with the flat statement that "woman's work and man's work are just anything they can do for each other" (505). Ultimately, Arthur discovers his error in interpreting her haircut, finally reading Beth's physical sacrifices correctly in some photographs taken of her by a male friend. Recognizing in her wasted physique the depth of her suffering on his behalf, he returns at the close of the novel, evidently to reestablish their fellowship. As Teresa Mangum notes, there is a "subversive message" in Grand's ending to *The Beth Book*: although permanently separated from Dan Maclure, Beth never succeeds in divorcing him; Arthur, approaching Beth on horseback, would, indeed, seem to be carrying "our imaginations beyond the boundaries of the conventional novel" in presenting himself as her apparent lover (191).

As in the case of Beth's self-denial on behalf of Arthur, Gertrude's sacrifices during Phyllis' final illness are her passage to fulfillment with her New Man, the kindly scientist, Lord Watergate. Having survived a beloved wife and witnessed Gertrude's retrieval of Phyllis from a life of adultery, Lord Watergate is marked out as Gertrude's logical life-partner. Quietly supporting her through Phyllis' illness, Lord Watergate forges a deep connection to Gertrude, extending his aid to her "in recognition of a natural human obligation" to help the suffering (182). Levy describes their fellowship as a piercing through of social falsehoods: having been together "in those rare moments of life when the elaborate paraphernalia of everyday intercourse is thrown aside; when soul looks straight into soul through no intervening veil," these two may shy away from casual conversation, but they are bonded for life, ending the novel in a happy marriage (182).

To finish her hero's journey well, Dix uses Leslie's broken engagement and retreat from London as a wake-up call that inspires Redgold to re-read his lover's behavior. Finally realizing what she has done for him, he dumps his Liberal MP, complete with charming niece, and arranges to spend sixth months abroad earning his own capital. At the end of this time, which Leslie uses to cement her success as a commercial artist, the two are reunited as lovers and equals; as Sally Ledger puts it, they plan "a radically reformed, more equitable, comradely kind of marriage" than Redgold had originally envisioned (58).

As Pearson and Pope write, "the true hero shatters the established order and creates the new community" (13). For Levy, Grand, and Dix, the New

Woman can be such a hero, if she embodies elements of both the warrior and the martyr archetypes. In the successful relationships—coupled with the complete physical recoveries—that these authors imagine for their female protagonists, they also counter the late-century stereotype of the New Woman as a sexless and "bespectacled, physically degenerate weakling" who could neither find love nor produce healthy children (Richardson and Willis 13). Beth, Leslie, and Gertrude all end their respective novels healthy and contented; Gertrude and Lord Watergate, in fact, have already produced "a stout person with rosy cheeks and stiff white petticoats" by their story's close (193). For these authors, the state of martyr-heroism is not a permanent one for the New Woman, but a phase through which she must pass before successfully completing her journey. Recognizing that *fin de siècle* British society is still a repressive place for women, Levy, Grand, and Dix make their female protagonists earn their authority to enter companionate relationships by running a gauntlet of physical and emotional trials. In doing so, they demonstrate that the New Woman is ready to work hard and make sacrifices to create a new, egalitarian brand of marriage, if only the New Man will step forward to join her, and above all, will learn to interpret and appreciate her efforts aright.

While Levy, Grand, and Dixon create hopeful images of self-supporting women, Ella Hepworth Dixon offers, instead, a cautionary tale. Dixon uses *The Story of a Modern Woman* to foreground the difficult side of life for independent women in late-century London. And how does she do this? By removing, one by one, the social supports upon which Mary leans. Orphaned from the start, Mary loses her friend Alison to a terrible fever, alienates her one loyal suitor, marries off her younger brother, and rejects Vincent Hemming's late bid to make her his mistress. Utterly alone, Mary ultimately decides to soldier on, but her final rejection of a suicidal impulse by no means constitutes a happy ending to this novel. Dixon's message is clear: if she is to be fulfilled, a "modern woman" living in London somehow must find fellowship there.

Works cited

Ardis, Ann L. *New Women, New Novels: Feminism and Early Modernism.* New Brunswick, NJ: Rutgers University Press, 1990.

Beckman, Linda Hunt. *Amy Levy: Her Life and Letters.* Athens, OH: Ohio University Press, 2000.

Dix, Gertrude. *The Image Breakers.* New York, NY: Frederick A. Stokes Company Publishers, 1900.

Dixon, Ella Hepworth. *The Story of a Modern Woman*. Ed. John Lucas; Intro. by Kate Flint. London, UK: Merlin Press Ltd., 1990.

"Fellowship." *Shorter Oxford English Dictionary, on Historical Principles*. Vol. 1, 5th ed. Oxford, UK: Oxford University Press, 2002. 940.

Gaskell, Elizabeth. *North and South*. New York, NY: Penguin Books, 2003.

Grand, Sarah. *The Beth Book: Being a Study of the Life of Elizabeth Caldwell Maclure A Woman of Genius*. Intro. by Elaine Showalter. New York, NY: The Dial Press, 1980.

Houghton, Walter E. *The Victorian Frame of Mind, 1830 – 1870*. New Haven, CT: Yale University Press, 1985. Originally published in 1957.

Ledger, Sally. *The New Woman: Fiction and Feminism at the* fin de siècle. New York, NY: Manchester University Press, 1997.

Levy, Amy. *The Romance of a Shop*. Ed. Susan David Bernstein. Orchard Park, NY: Broadview Press, 2006.

Mangum, Teresa. *Married, Middlebrow, and Militant: Sarah Grand and the New Woman Novel*. Ann Arbor, MI: The University of Michigan Press, 1998.

Marks, Patricia. *Bicycles, Bangs, and Bloomers: The New Woman in the Popular Press*. Lexington, KY: The University Press of Kentucky, 1990.

Nord, Deborah Epstein. *Walking the Victorian Streets: Women, Representation, and the City*. Ithaca, NY: Cornell University Press, 1995.

Parsons, Deborah L. *Streetwalking the Metropolis: Women, the City, and Modernity*. New York, NY: Oxford University Press, 2000.

Pearson, Carol S. *The Hero Within: Six Archetypes We Live By*. San Francisco, CA: Harper & Row Publishers, 1989.

Pearson, Carol S., and Katherine Pope. *The Female Hero in American and British Literature*. New York, NY: R. R. Bowker Company, 1981.

Reynolds, Kimberley and Nicola Humble. *Victorian Heroines: Representations of Femininity in Nineteenth-Century Literature and Art*. New York, NY: Harvester Wheatsheaf, 1993.

Richardson, Angelique, and Chris Willis. "Introduction." *The New Woman in Fiction and in Fact:* Fin-de-Siècle *Feminisms*. Ed. Angelique Richardson and Chris Willis. Foreward by Lyn Pykett. New York, NY: Palgrave Publishers Ltd, 2001. 1 – 38.

Schaffer, Talia. "'Nothing But Foolscap and Ink': Inventing the New Woman." *The New Woman in Fiction and in Fact:* Fin-de-Siecle

Feminisms. Angelique Richardson and Chris Willis, Eds. New York, NY: Palgrave Publishers Ltd., 2001. 39 – 52.

Notes

[1] For a pithy explanation of some of the discursive uses of the New Woman image, see Talia Schaffer's "'Nothing But Foolscap and Ink': Inventing the New Woman" in *The New Woman in Fiction and in Fact: Fin-de-Siécle Feminisms,*" edited by Angelique Richardson and Chris Willis (London: Palgrave Publishers Ltd., 2001), Chapter 1. Deborah Nord's *Walking the Victorian Streets: Women, Representation, and the City* (Ithaca, NY: Cornell University Press, 1995) describes the lives and writings of three New Women—Amy Levy, Margaret Harkness, and Beatrice Webb—in her sixth chapter, "'Neither Pairs Nor Odd'": Women, Urban Community, and Writing in the 1880s." Sally Ledger's excellent *The New Woman: Fiction and Feminism at the* fin de siecle (New York, NY: Manchester University Press, 1997) discusses a wide variety of discursive representations of New Womanhood.

[2] See Chapter Five, "Crossing the Line: Figuring Revolutions" in Ardis's important *New Women, New Novels: Feminism and Early Modernism* (New Brunswick, NJ: Rutgers University Press, 1990).

[3] See Ledger's chapter entitled "The New Woman and emergent lesbian identity" in *The New Woman: Fiction and Feminism in the* fin de siècle.

[4] In the case of Sarah Grand's novel *The Beth Book*, a detailed *künstelrroman*, the London scenes appear in the final third of the novel, but are, nonetheless, important parts of the storyline.

[5] Leslie Ardent is actually one of two co-protagonists in *The Image Breakers*. See Ann Ardis' *New Women, New Novels* for a detailed reading of Rosalind Dangerfield, Dix's other central New Woman character.

[6] Pearson and Pope purposely use the term "female hero" because they see the term "heroine" as designating "a secondary, supporting character in a man's story" (18). I am following their lead and using the term "hero" as well.

[7] As Ann Ardis has argued, Leslie and Rosalind do develop a mutually-sustaining friendship in the course of the novel, coming to "depend upon each other" for support through their various trials as progressive women (134). This friendship begins as very lopsided in terms of power, though: Rosalind is older and more world-wise than Leslie, and she tries to use her influence over the younger woman to make Leslie stay with her against her wishes in a socialist commune. Even when Leslie has established her independence and taken a lover, Rosalind refuses to accept her life decisions, criticizing her choice of men and condemning her sexual relationship as an "aberration" and a "danger" to her well-being (Dix 275).

[8] See Sally Ledger's chapter entitled "The New Woman in the modern city" for a sustained discussion of the late-century woman as modern *flâneuse.*

CHAPTER SEVEN

DISPOSING OF THE BODY:
LITERARY AUTHORITY, FEMALE DESIRE
AND THE REVERSE KUNSTLERROMAN
OF RHODA BROUGHTON'S
A FOOL IN HER FOLLY

TAMAR HELLER

Near the end of Rhoda Broughton's last, posthumously published novel *A Fool in Her Folly* (1920)—set in the mid-Victorian period in which she herself came of age—an aspiring writer violently destroys her own manuscript. In a climactic scene Char Hankey, the clergyman's daughter who is Broughton's protagonist and narrator, "rend[s] and tear[s]" her first, and only, work of fiction, a tale of adulterous passion entitled *LOVE*:

> Scissors, knife, frenzied fingers, I called in, and seized everything within my reach, to aid me . . . I would   have reduced it to powder, to finest dust, had I been able! As I tore, I tried not to read; but do what I would— shut my eyes, even—horrible sentences stood out, and seemed to grin at and jibe me like embodied devils! (342-43)

Char is not the first horrified reader of her novel to "annihilate the accursed thing" (342); her parents had already burned an earlier draft discovered by a prying governess. Unlike Broughton, who weathered attacks on the morality of her first novels, *Not Wisely but Too Well* and *Cometh Up as a Flower* (both published in 1867), to enjoy a fifty-three year career as "Queen of the Circulating Libraries," Char cannot, finally, surmount obstacles to authorship that include, in addition to the incineration of her manuscript, exile to the home of a widowed aunt until she promises never to write again.

Significantly, however, the final blow to her career comes from Char herself. Rebelliously rewriting *LOVE* at her aunt's house, she destroys the new draft upon discovering the perfidy of Bill Drinkwater, a rakish young man with whom she had fallen in love upon her arrival. Having modeled the hero of her reconstructed novel on Drinkwater—and herself being almost seduced by him in the process—Char is devastated to learn that his amorous attentions were only a ruse to allow him to press unwanted attentions on her aunt. Overcome by "shame and mortification" at her confusion of art and life, Char gives her parents the required oath to renounce authorship and shreds the manuscript that represents at once "the fabric of my ambition and my love" (343). Describing her novel as an amalgam of literary aspirations and desire, Char makes the same connection between sexuality and textuality as when she likens the sentences she destroys to "embodied devils." Even her clandestine disposal of the shredded pages underscores this metonymy of body and text; flinging open the window of the train on her way home, she rids herself of "the fragments of Fulke and Eleanora" (348), her adulterous protagonists.

In this essay I explore the imbrication of bodies, texts, and female linguistic authority in Broughton's valedictory portrait of the artist as a young woman. Given the autobiographical parallels between Broughton and Char—both clergymen's daughters who write sensation fiction— Shirley Jones finds it "curious[]" that in her final novel Broughton dooms her heroine to a professional disaster she herself evaded (209). Ironically, by implying Char is a "fool" for writing *LOVE*—and for living its fantasy of female desire—Broughton assumes the role of moralistic censor of sensationalism taken by critics such as Margaret Oliphant, who famously attacked the "fleshly, unlovely record of the feminine soul" in Broughton's early fiction. Despite her own literary success, then, Broughton reproduces the Victorian stereotype of female sensation writers corrupting impressionable girls. At the same time, however, in its depiction of the narrow-minded opposition Char encounters in her literary efforts, *A Fool in Her Folly* indicts rather than endorses Victorian parochialism. In this sense, Broughton's metafictional last novel is a record of her ambivalence about female authorship, simultaneously chastising female literary ambition and critiquing that chastisement to suggest that young women need greater scope for their professional talents than that afforded by traditional domesticity.

To the extent that it critiques Victorian domestic ideology, *A Fool in Her Folly* has strong affinities with the New Woman Kunstlerroman, a genre so common in the works of such *fin-de-siècle* feminists as Sarah

Grand, Mona Caird, Ella Hepworth Dixon, and George Egerton that some critics have identified it as the quintessential New Woman narrative. [1] Featuring, as Lyn Pykett says, "would-be literary artists, painters, and musicians who break down or give in under the pressures of the various circumstances which conspire against them" (136), the New Woman Kunstlerroman could more be accurately be described as a reverse Kunstlerroman, in which the woman artist fails, rather than succeeds, in becoming a professional in her chosen field. The episode in which Char's parents consign their daughter's manuscript to the flames echoes the climax of that "classic text of New Woman fiction," as Linda Peterson calls it, Mary Cholmondeley's *Red Pottage* (1899), in which a hidebound clergyman burns the only draft of his sister's brilliantly iconoclastic novel (see Peterson,"The Role of Periodicals" 33).

    That Broughton was the younger Cholmondeley's friend and mentor—and moreover expressed "sympathy and kindly feeling" in her comments on *Red Pottage* (*Kindred Hands* 112)—makes it likely that the plot similarities between Cholmondeley's work and *A Fool in Her Folly* are not accidental. Yet, as the anxieties about female authorship in *A Fool in Her Folly* suggest, Broughton is by no means so unambiguously feminist as New Women of a younger generation. In several novels, in fact, Broughton is even reactionary in her response to the New Woman: *Dear Faustina* (1897) recalls her friend Henry James's *The Bostonians* in its depiction of the unhealthy relationship—complete with lesbian overtones—between a sinister feminist and a naïve young woman, while the disastrous experiences of a New Woman writer in *A Beginner* (1894) anticipate the reverse Kunstlerroman of Broughton's last novel. Even these satires of New Women, however, are not wholly conservative. Though chastising the sinister feminist, *Dear Faustina* ends—like a New Woman novel—with the heroine deferring marriage so she can do settlement work; moreover, as Pamela Gilbert points out, the heroine's destruction of her avant-garde novel in *A Beginner* may be greater proof of her inability to withstand critical opposition than it is to her own lack of literary potential (129).

    Thus, even while noting similarities between her fiction and that of New Women writers, it is important to remember the generational divide that separated Broughton from younger, more radical feminists such as George Egerton. In the history of changing gender roles and sexual attitudes Broughton is a transitional figure who, as Walter Sichel commented in 1917, "spans the distance between the 'Girl of the Period' and the New Woman" (Wood 116). Beginning her career as a "novelist of revolt" whose passionate, unconventional heroines rivaled those of

Charlotte Brontë and George Eliot (*Spectator* 1173), by the end of her life Broughton was to joke about how tame her work appeared to a younger generation. In *A Fool in Her* Folly Char occupies a similarly anachronistic position; eighty at the time of her narration—and thus Broughton's age at her death—she constantly refers to changes in sexual attitudes since her girlhood, noting, for example, that the naughty novels of her youth would seem mere "pap" to the "strong-stomached maidens of today" (15). Moreover, Char reminds her presumably younger audience that her parents' generation admitted of no "alternative to marriage as a career for their daughters" (8). As an elderly commentator on changes in women's status since the Victorian period, Char takes the same position as Broughton herself in "Girls Past and Present ," an essay published in the same year—1920—as *A Fool in Her Folly*, and a useful companion piece to the novel in its ambivalent response to changes in sexual mores between the Victorian and the post-World War I periods. In "Girls Past and Present" Broughton applauds how "The girl of 1920 does a great deal more and suffers a great deal less than her elder sisters of the fifties and sixties of last century . . . No check stands in the way of her guiding every faculty of her being into whatever channel she feels the inclination or the ability to direct them" (38 c.1). At the same time, however, Broughton wonders if there was not something to be said for the "decent mystery of yesterday," so different from the "brazen candor" of the flapper "about whose heart and sentiments there is as little mystery as about her almost undraped body" (141 c.1).

In the remainder of this essay I will examine the mixed ideological messages in Broughton's last novel that—like her ambivalent response to shifts in sexual attitudes in "Girls Past and Present"—cause the text on one hand to contain the unruly energies of female texts and female bodies, while, on the other hand, undercutting its own conservative didacticism. Indeed, in keeping with its backward glance to the Victorian age, *A Fool in Her Folly* recalls the "doubletalk" that Sandra Gilbert and Susan Gubar associate with the Victorian woman writer, who, they claim, typically hides a subversive message beneath a more conventional one (*Madwoman* 74-75). Not only are there ways in which Char's narrative begs to be read against the grain of its apparent message about the "folly" of female authorship, but the novel prefigures Virginia Woolf's portrait of the woman writer battling the Angel in the House in its analysis of how women internalize ideologies that limit their creativity and, in the process, prevent them from writing freely about the female body and its desires.

"Crushed and Humiliated": Deauthorizing the Female Sensation Writer

In her introduction to *A Fool in Her Folly,* Broughton's friend Marie Belloc Lowndes was not surprised that Char, unlike her creator, ends up "crushed and humiliated" (350) in her efforts to become a "second Charlotte Brontë" (11). Recalling how "curiously humble" Broughton was about her literary talents (6), Lowndes situates the novel's plot of the failed woman writer in the "Victorian tradition" of considering "professional authorship as not at all suitable for ladies" (6). Broughton, Lowndes claims, "was content to regard her literary gift as a kind of elegant accomplishment" (6) instead of as a profession.[2] Indeed, publishing her first three novels anonymously, Broughton, like many women of her generation, initially eschewed public identification as an author.

In the past several decades feminist scholarship has commented extensively on the connection made by Victorians between women publishing in the public sphere and prostitution; as Catherine Gallagher claims, in the Victorian era the woman writer is often depicted as a "composite image of usurer and whore" (44). Publically purveying tales of transgressive female desire, the female sensation writer was particularly associated with erotic commodification. In *A Fool in Her Folly*, the intersection between sensationalism, commodification, and the female body is evident from the opening lines. Char begins her narrative by claiming that her earliest memory is of a working-class man calling out to her as she walked to church that her garter was coming off (7). She also recalls an incident some years later in which "a ruffian of the same class as the earlier one shouted to me from the top of a hay wain, `You're losing your ribbons, my dear'" (7).

Foreshadowing the impropriety of Char's authoring a tale of adulterous passion, these introductory anecdotes underscore the parallel between Char's body and that of her text. For Char to publish *LOVE* would, presumably, be equivalent to removing her clothes before a lower-class audience—an image that not only underscores the resemblance between female sensation writer and prostitute, but also reflects the association of sensation fiction with newly publicized accounts of sexual deviance. Barbara Leckie has examined how the flood of newspaper coverage of Divorce Court cases in the 1860s—made possible by the change in divorce law effected by the 1857 Matrimonial Causes Act—gave rise to the type of cultural anxieties also evoked by sensation fiction; indeed, by drawing heavily on journalistic sources to shape its own exposés of domestic deviance, sensationalism, like newspapers, made public information

hitherto considered inappropriate for a middle-class female audience.[3]
This public dissemination of sexual knowledge through journalistic and
fictional discourses destabilizes class as well as gender hierarchies,
subjecting the middle-class woman's domestic secrets to a display before a
cross-class audience reminiscent of a strip show.

The link between the public display of the female body and potential
class degradation is underscored by Char's experience working on the first
draft of *LOVE*. Having just penned a love scene between her protagonists
Fulke and Eleanora, Char learns from her youngest sibling that her mother
and elder, married sister have been sharing "secrets" about a real-life
tragedy of unrequited passion:

> "They were talking about that poor still-room maid at the Abbey who
> drowned herself in the mere last Thursday. It seems that she did it for love
> of Tom Beach, who had jilted her; and then Harriet lowered her voice and
> said something about a baby." (35)

Aware that she has stumbled upon "one of these naked violent love
dramas, my total lack of acquaintance with which had been such a clog
and fetter upon the wings of my imagination" (35), Char reads the dead
maid's suicide note in—most significantly—a newspaper. While noting
class markers of "faulty grammar" and "wildly phonetic orthography,"
Char is nonetheless so struck by the "shriek of mad passion, revolt, and
despair" of the "poor still-room maid's `Oh, God! Jim, 'ow could you?'"
(41) that she acknowledges the poverty of her own efforts. Indeed,
ashamed of her "miserable, artificial, flat performance," Char destroys the
speech she has just written and resolves to revise it based on her new
knowledge of unrequited love. By modeling her heroine's expressions of
desire on those of a working-class woman, Char herself becomes
associated, as she had when working-class men had commented on her
clothes coming off, with what is "lower" in the body politic.

Such a blurring of class identities recalls Susan Bernstein's point that
critics saw sensation fiction "inciting `lower and more animal instincts'
associated with the underclass and the primitive" (223) in middle-class
female readers. Significantly, too, the still-maid's story involves the
evasion of motherhood. While Char does not find out, or at least does not
reveal, all details of the maid's "illegitimate love" (36), the tale, by
including a baby, is presumably in some sense a narrative of infanticide,
whether the maid killed herself upon learning that she was pregnant or
murdered a newborn infant before committing suicide. By showing
women—often, like Eliot's Hetty Sorrel, of working-class origin—
pursuing sexual activity but rejecting maternity, nineteenth-century

fictional and journalistic narratives represent infanticide as an attack on middle-class values embodied in domestic ideology's idealization of the mother.[4]

Providing Char with a knowledge of illicit sexuality she would not otherwise have acquired, the still-maid's tale thus functions as an image for the social contamination associated in the nineteenth century both with prostitution and sensationalism. Lynda Nead has shown how, in the Victorian period, the prostitute's body became the locus of anxieties about disease infiltrating all classes of society (118-34); similarly, critics of sensationalism tended to depict the genre as a contagion that, invading the bodies of middle- and upper-class female readers with what Margaret Oliphant called "forbidden knowledge" (174), reduces them to the same level as streetwalkers. In the famous critique of sensation fiction in *Blackwood's* which targeted *Cometh Up as a Flower* as an example of the "abomination among us," Margaret Oliphant portrays the relationship between female writer and reader of sensationalism as a type of erotic contagion:

> [I]t is women who describe those sensuous raptures . . . this eagerness of physical sensation, is represented as the natural sentiment of English girls . . . . It is a shame to women so to write; and is a shame to the women who read and accept as a true representation of themselves and their ways the equivocal talk and fleshly inclinations herein attributed to them. (175, 187, Maunder vers.)

Char resembles the young female reader trained, as Oliphant had said, to believe that "eagerness of physical sensation" is "natural" after ingesting novels in which women "give and receive burning kisses and frantic embraces, and live in a voluptuous dream" (175). Seduced by her own story of passion, Char fills the roles both of author and audience of sensationalism, her own desiring body and the body of her text about desire increasingly conflated. Emboldened by her novel's apotheosis of love as the "greatest thing in the world" (79), Char propels herself with "immodest eagerness" (338) into the arms of the unsavory Drinkwater. When, on one occasion, the young man presses "hot" lips to her wrist, Char claims that "all the nice and modest conventions of which I had been reared rolled back on my mind, and the fact that stung me most sharply was the knowledge that I was tingling with the thrill born of that caress" (228, 229). At one point her romantic fantasies even lead Char to enter a deserted shepherd's hut with Drinkwater and stay there three hours—the type of assignation that could easily ruin her reputation. Moreover, during this meeting, she exchanges with Drinkwater both "torrid endearments"

(293) and passionate embraces, all the while naïvely assuming he wishes to marry her. Luck alone—or some lingering vestige of conscience on Drinkwater's part—preserves her from becoming a fallen woman. As it is, only years later is she "fully aware by how near a shave I had escaped the greatest peril to which I had ever been, or was ever likely to be, exposed" (297).

Not only does Char's narrow escape from sexual fall illustrate Oliphant's point about the threat to female chastity posed by sensationalism, but, like Oliphant's remarks themselves, this plot evokes a longstanding didactic tradition—exemplified by such works as *The Female Quixote* and *Northanger Abbey*—of warning young girls of the consequences of consuming romantic fiction. In this sense, *A Fool in Her Folly* is as much about the perils of women's reading as it is about the folly of their writing. In the novel's first chapters Char details how, through forays in the well-stocked family library, she came to acquire her "uncanny and unseemly book knowledge" (228):

> What a brazier was Byron! How I scorched my virginal soul at his furnace fires! , , , Could I have said anything but a raptured 'Yes' to Shelley if he had asked me to 'come away,' even had it been from an excellent husband, as in the case of Jane Williams? (20)

Although Char respects her parents' restrictions on certain volumes, she devours others that would presumably make their hair stand on end—a manipulation of the rules only possible because she possesses more literary knowledge than her censors. For example, she skips the "long row of Bowdlers" to explore the books nearest them on the shelves, "unexpurgated Ben Jonsons, Websters, and Fords . . . whose perniciousness was unsuspected because they were never opened save by me" (22). As Char says,

> *The Heart of Midlothian* was—incredible as it now seems—on our "Index." But of what use to ban that great *Heart* from the perusal of a person who took *Tom Jones* to bed with her, who was intimately acquainted with most of the *grandes amoreuses* of French eighteenth-century literature?

Char's wording humorously implies the combined bodily and textual transgression of taking *Tom Jones* "to bed with her," as well as being "intimately acquainted" with French narratives of illicit passion. Once again, transgressive books and the female body are coupled in a kind of textual intercourse. Moreover, this textual intercourse enables Char to define her own linguistic authority: as Kate Flint claims, reading is "centrally bound in with questions of authority . . . authority to speak, to write, to define, to manage, and to change not just the institutions of literature, but those of society itself" (43).[5] Augmenting her slender knowledge of sexuality through her reading, Char makes her representation of desire that much more persuasive and compelling.

Broughton's account of Char's forays in the family library may be one of the novel's most autobiographical sections. Yet, by undercutting her heroine's authority as reader and writer, Broughton rewrites the history of her own early career, in which she made heavy use of her voluminous reading in order to enhance her literary status. Broughton's first two novels, *Not Wisely but Too Well* and *Cometh Up as a Flower*, are particularly rich in allusions to a dizzying array of both fictional and nonfictional texts. While such obsessive citations have been seen as evidence of Broughton's pedantry, more recently critics have read them as an attempt, given the low cultural prestige of sensationalism, to lay claim to as much cultural capital as possible, including allusions to works by such canonical male writers as Pope, Tennyson, and Shakespeare.[6] As her career progressed, Broughton's self-deprecating attitude toward her work suggests she came to acquiesce to its classification as ephemeral popular— and feminine—entertainment, a classification that reflected the growing divide between "highbrow" and "lowbrow" literature fostered by such male authors as Broughton's self-canonizing friend Henry James.[7]

At the same time, however, in her last novel Broughton attempts to position herself in a tradition of higher-status, or at least influential, women's writing. Not only does Char declare she wishes to become a "second Charlotte Brontë" (11), but *A Fool in Her Folly* recalls the plots of several Austen novels. I have already mentioned *Northanger Abbey* as a possible source, but Char's misreading of Drinkwater's character also recalls Elizabeth Bennett's similar discovery regarding Wickham in *Pride and Prejudice*, or the literary Marianne's jilting by Willoughby in *Sense and Sensibility*. In one sense, the similarities between *A Fool in Her Folly* and Austenian narrative augments Broughton's literary status, and, indeed, in her introduction to *A Fool in Her Folly* Lowndes claims that Broughton was "the nearest thing in spirit to Jane Austen that we have had in recent times" (5). Yet the telos of the Austenian narrative of moral education requires Char to abandon authorship and, in consequence, to contain the subversive sexuality of herself and her potential female readers. When she destroys her manuscript at the novel's end, she presumably does so in order to avoid what Oliphant had accused Broughton and other female sensationalists of doing, disseminating inappropriately explicit material to girls as gullible as herself.

"Murdering My Offspring": Battling the Maternal Angel

As proof she has learned her lesson about the dangers of romance, when Char marries a year after her parents' deaths she claims that she "might have employed the phrase of George Whitefield, who, when proposing marriage to his future wife, added that he thanked God that there was not the slightest mixture of carnal love in his feeling for her" (352). Yet so hyperbolic is Char's avoidance of romance that Broughton seems to be poking fun not only at her heroine's attempts at authorship but her repentance as well. Here, the sense of humor Broughton shares with Jane Austen renders ambiguous the moral of Char's story. On one hand, the novel's determinedly light tone contributes to the lack of seriousness it accords female authorship. But Broughton's gently irreverent humor also emphasizes her satiric distance from Victorian values. So proper does Char become following her adventures that she parodies Victorian maidenhood: "'a good, conscientious girl, dull, but rather pretty,' was the verdict of my acquaintances" (351). Finally, then, Char makes herself into a Victorian artifact reminiscent of other antiquated customs of the period, like the chaperone, which are now "deader than the dodo!" (9). As Shirley Jones says, in her narratorial comments the older Char underscores the "historically specific" nature of her experience, implying that her story is finally "a curiosity" rather than a tale relevant to the present moment (230). Indeed, Broughton's pointed reminders of the outdatedness of Victorian customs implies that her heroine may well have been over-hasty in accepting their restrictions, and thus lacks the resilience of her sturdier creator.

Broughton's portrayal of Char's parents is a particularly vivid example of how the novel's critique of Victorian values competes with its chastisement of the heroine's ambition. Although Char eventually accepts her father's evaluation of *LOVE* as "pestilent balderdash" (81), his conduct, and that of her mother, after reading their daughter's manuscript without her permission does not cast them in a positive light. As I argued earlier, the bonfire of Char's manuscript is almost certainly an allusion to Mary Cholmondeley's devastating indictment of Victorian parochialism in *Red Pottage*. Indeed, in accusing her parents of "murdering my offspring" (89), Char uses the same metaphor as Cholmondeley's Hester as she explains the magnitude of his offense to the clergyman-brother who destroys her manuscript: "'When Regie was ill,' said the slow difficult voice, 'I did what I could. I did not let your child die. Why have you killed mine?'" (276). When Char laments that her parents have burned "the offspring of *my* heart and brain—so much dearer, so far more precious, than any mere child of the flesh could ever be" (89), she, like Hester, emphasizes her proto-New Woman rejection of domestic ideology in favor of intellectual activity. Broughton thus underscores the frequent tension between women's artistry and maternity, a subject not only addressed by Cholmondeley's image of the book as surrogate child, but more extensively examined in New Woman fiction such as Elizabeth Stuart Phelps's *The Story of Avis*, Mona Caird's *The Daughters of Danaus*, and George Egerton's short stories which, as Nichole Fluhr argues, consistently "interrogat[es] the cultural opposition between women's writing and mothering" (245).

Thus, when Char compares her destroyed manuscript to a baby, the infanticide narrative implied in the still-room maid's story has shifted its ideological register, functioning not as an image for the problematic evasion of maternity but, instead, for the injustice of denying women access to professional occupations. Tellingly, when Char's parents demand she never write again, Char angrily claims "they had no right to demand of me the sacrifice of my career" (207). Indeed, by employing a first-person voice, Broughton makes it more likely that her readers will empathize with her heroine's rebellion against parental tyranny. Such empathy is particularly likely if we are the post-Victorian audience to whom the narrative is directed, and who, unlike Char's contemporaries, no longer find the idea that "a couple of girls should find an affinity in each other . . . and, 'forsaking all other,' betake themselves to a joint flat, to maintain which their own industries should furnish the means" a notion that "would have consigned the holder of it to Bedlam" (9).

We may, indeed, come to see Char's story as an example of how hard it is, finally, for even a rebellious Victorian daughter wholly to reject the ideology in which she was raised, a theme that also informs the essay I mentioned earlier, "Girls Past and Present." Approving the expanded professional opportunities open to a younger generation of women as she does in this essay, Broughton is still disconcerted by the post-World War I period's "rampant virgin." Yet she also admits that

> It is very difficult for one with that natural bias toward the past which comes with old age to judge impartially an alien world, an "alien" which to ancient eyes has a tendency to appear an "undesirable" one. It is only with an effort that one can lay prepossession and prejudice aside, can free oneself from the standards, toss aside the weights and measures of one's youth; but if one can succeed in doing so, one is forced to confess that the girl of 1920 is a larger, more useful, and happier being than was her grandmother[.] (141 c.3).

In other words, Broughton insightfully acknowledges how ideology works to colonize the minds even of those who try to resist it. Although she rebelled against many of the values with which she was indoctrinated, Broughton still necessarily sees the world differently from the "new woman," who, if she "lacks the fragrant grace, the modesty and reverence for household ties and sanctities of her predecessor . . . is not in the least aware of it and so is not a penny the worse off!" (141 c.3).

In *A Fool in Her Folly*, Broughton dramatizes the difficulty of putting aside Victorian "prepossession and prejudice" through Char's mixed feelings toward her all-too-Victorian mother. "Inveterately pleasant," Char's mother is a "Haus Engel" (21) who embodies the spirit of domestic ideology. Linking the mother/daughter plot and that of the female reader, one of the novel's more amusing scenes takes place in the family library as Char dupes her mother so she cannot appropriately monitor her daughter's reading choices. Capitalizing, in fact, on her mother's proper ignorance of improper knowledge, Char responds to her query about the novel she is currently reading—*Manon Lescaut*—by describing it as "only a little book by a man called the Abbé Prévost" (21). Reassured by the author's clerical credentials, even if he is a "Papist" (21), Char's mother approves her daughter's choice, leaving Char uncomfortably aware she has not told the entire truth about her risqué reading. Recollecting her mother leaving the library, Char memorializes the Victorian period's genteel feminine ideal: "I can see her now, passing through the door, in a Prussian blue barege dress, with a Honiton lace cap on her brown hair, and a little gold chatelaine gently jingling at her side" (22).

On one hand, Char's memory of her mother is tinged with affectionate nostalgia. On the other hand, though, in her serene ignorance of the intellectual world Char's mother appears distressingly simple-minded. Moreover, in her daughter's hour of need, when Char begs her on her knees to return the manuscript, her mother "turned away" (86), a symbolic rejection of her daughter's professional aspirations that further fuels the hitherto dutiful girl's "sullen fire of revolt" (93). Throughout the novel, Char both rebels against and continues to be influenced by her mother's old-fashioned values. At a critical moment in exile at her aunt's, when she first thinks of reconstructing her destroyed manuscript, "Before me, in the light of the papers, seemed to rise the face of mamma, sadder and severer than I had ever seen it with bodily eyes" (187). So guilt-stricken is Char by this maternal super-ego that she is unable to write following its appearance. Appropriately disembodied, the mother's presence thus stifles the daughter's attempt to write about the body.

Broughton's portrayal of the angelic mother who disables her daughter's literary expression anticipates Virginia Woolf's treatment of this theme in *To the Lighthouse*, which traces the attempts of the New Woman artist Lily Briscoe to escape the legacy of that quintessential domestic woman, Mrs. Ramsey. Similarly, in her 1931 essay "Professions for Women," Woolf describes, in a memorably hilarious psychomachia, her own victory over the internalized ghost of the Victorian Angel in the House who embodies the ideology of female self-effacement as well as its accompanying sexual repressiveness. As Woolf sits down to review a book by a famous man, the Angel "made as if to guide my pen," urging the young woman to tone down her criticism of men and to censor explicit references to sexuality: "Never let anybody guess that you have a mind of your own. Above all, be pure" (59). "Had I not killed her," Woolf claims, "she would have killed me. She would have plucked the heart out of my writing" (59).

Elsewhere in the essay Woolf sees her defeat of the angel as the necessary precondition for her to write freely about sex, or, as she puts it, "the truth about my own experiences as a body" (62). Yet, admitting that she has not yet reached this last goal, Woolf may not, finally, have banished the maternal super-ego and its messages about chastity as triumphantly as she claims. She thus may not be as different as she wishes from a Victorian daughter like Char, to whom killing the angel is even more difficult than it was for a woman of a younger generation.[8] Char cannot extricate herself from the guilt-tripping snares cast by her mother, who in her letters to her daughter at Aunt Florinda's "seemed to be throwing out tendrils of mother-love to wind around and clasp me" (103). Indeed, upon Char's return home, she records the first sight of her mother waiting to greet her with an ecstasy that eclipses all previous passions: "*one* figure in front of all the others! . . . For how long was I clasped in its arms? How much later was it that I was kneeling at that figure's feet . . . was embracing its knees?" (350).

Her rapturous reunion with her mother is not the only sign that Char has not yet freed herself from Victorian values. Even her supposedly transgressive infatuation is structured by the guiding premise of domestic ideology, that women function as spiritual guides to men. Pamela-like, Char sees it as her "holy task" (326) to reform, and then marry, the rakish Drinkwater, notions of which she is painfully disabused. As I have claimed, Broughton's portrayal of Char's confusion of romance-reading with life, and her abdication of literary authority in consequence, undoubtedly has conservative elements. Yet we can also see Drinkwater and Char's aborted relationship as an example of the evasion of the romance plot's traditional closure in Broughton's work more generally. I have argued elsewhere, for instance, that Broughton's decision at the end of the triple-decker version of *Not Wisely but Too Well* to make her heroine an Anglican nun laboring in the London slums is an attempt to imagine an independent role for women outside marriage ("'That Muddy, Polluted Flood'" 97-98). Moreover, the topos of women misled by romantic conventions is not only to be found in the work of writers seeking to limit female autonomy. Indeed, since eighteenth- and nineteenth-century feminists argued that marriage itself limited female freedom, one could warn, as did Mary Wollstonecraft, that romantic discourses brainwash women into accepting relationships in which they are men's property rather than their equals.[9] Many of Broughton's novels contain a Wollstonecraftian analysis of how women's disadvantaged economic position pressures them to marry; this is most the notably the case in her early sensation fiction, *Cometh Up as a Flower*, in which the penniless heroine's selling "so many pounds of [her] prime white flesh" (400) in a mercenary match echoes the Wollstonecraftian description of marriage as "legal prostitution" for women denied the ability to support themselves by their own labors (*Vindication* 148).[10]

To note that Broughton's work has affinities with Wollstonecraftian feminism is not, of course, to minimize the conservative elements of her fiction. Kate Chester's penitential fate in *Not Wisely*, for example, as well as the heroine's death in *Cometh Up* following a failed attempt to flee her stifling marriage, are to some extent a nod to Victorian conventions against allowing transgressive women to live happily ever after. Yet Broughton's persistent refusal to imagine marriage as, in the words of the narrator of *Not Wisely*, "the main plot of a woman's life" (49) is in keeping with the critique of male exploitation of women both in her sensation fiction and her later works. In this sense, Broughton's evasion of the telos of romantic fulfillment could be seen as attempting what she sees the twentieth century finally accomplishing, finding professional alternatives for women to what she calls in "Girls Past and Present" the "nuptial yoke" (141 c.3).

That Char worships Drinkwater as the "lord and governor" (299) to whom her life is to be "a burnt offering" (311) is thus troubling evidence of her conventional willingness to subordinate her will to that of a man. Char should be warned against marital immolation by the example of her aunt Florinda, recovering from twenty years of "married hell" (164) to a husband described as a "perfect monster": "There was no insult or brutality to which he did not subject her . . . he used to hale her about by the hair of her head" (170). Even after the "gyves and manacles" of her marriage (203) are removed by her husband's death, Aunt Florinda cannot escape subjugation to men. She develops a Platonic relationship with a Mr. Delaval, the heir to her husband's estate, a relationship in which "so nice and vigilant an observation as he directed towards my aunt's every word, action, and—one might almost say—thought, constituted a tyranny, though undoubtedly a beneficent one" (271).[11] Given how susceptible Aunt Florinda is to male control, it is telling that Drinkwater is in love with her rather than with her niece; presumably he can more easily imagine Florinda as an object of sexual domination. Ominously, in the scene in which Char meets Drinkwater in the shepherd's hut, he "forced me into his embrace with an almost brutality which squeezed the life out of me" (298), suggesting that he, like Aunt Florinda's former husband, possesses a capacity for abuse. Fortunately Drinkwater's stalking of Aunt Florinda—who has endured more than enough already—is unsuccessful, and he departs town after leaving an agonized confession of his love for her aunt that Delaval shows Char as evidence of his duplicity.

Under these circumstances, we might see Char's escape from Drinkwater's clutches as fortunate. Yet, having renounced simultaneously "my ambition and my love" (343), Char—not having the £500 a year and a room of her own that Woolf claims the woman artist requires—returns to the role of unmarried daughter and nurse of her elderly parents, a post she only exchanges for that of wife to a husband for whom she feels no passion but who is "glaringly in need of care" (352). Char's exchange of one type of stifling domesticity for another is the kind of fate Broughton, in "Girls Past and Present," sees women of a younger generation finally avoiding:

> Marriage—in the Victorian age practically the only means of escape from a home bondage prolonged to an age when "the whole head was sick and the whole heart faint"—is to many of the girls of to-day an unessential accident, which may or may not happen to them, but which in any case cannot materially affect the serious business of their lives, their professional or political activities. (38 c. 1)

Born too early for this transformation of women's options—an improvement that would have a striking impact on the lives of women writers—Char concludes her narration claiming "there is nothing left for me but to die. I hope that I shall do it decently" (352). With these lines, *A Fool in Her Folly* envisions the passing of the old order, of the would-be female intellectuals of the Victorian age who wished for a life outside domesticity but were themselves unable to attain it. Broughton suggests that it will be for a younger generation to carry on the revolution which she, unlike the defeated novelist Char, helped to initiate, that of imagining a world in which women would not be accused of "folly" for writing—or living—unconventional plots.

Works cited

Ardis, Ann. *New Women, New Novels: Feminism and Early Modernism.* New Brunswick: Rutgers UP, 1990.
—. "'Retreat with Honour': Mary Cholmondeley's Presentation of the New Woman As Artist in *Red Pottage*." *Writing the Woman Artist: Essays on Poetics, Politics, and Portraiture.* Ed. Suzanne W. Jones. Philadelphia: U of Pennsylvania P, 1991. 333-50.
Bernstein, Susan. "Dirty Reading: Sensation Fiction, Women, and Primitivism." *Criticism* 36.2 (Spring 1994): 213-41.
Black, Helen C. *Notable Women Authors of the Day.* 1893. Essay Index Reprint Series. Freeport, New York: Books for Libraries, Press, 1972.
Broughton, Rhoda. *A Beginner.* 1894. N.p.: Elibron Classics, 2005.
—. *A Fool in Her Folly.* Introd. Marie Belloc Lowndes. London: Odhams Press, 1920.
—. *Cometh Up as a Flower.* Ed. Tamar Heller. *Varieties of Women's Sensation Fiction.* Gen. ed. Andrew Maunder. Vol. 4b. London: Pickering and Chatto, 2004.
—. *Dear Faustina.* London: Bentley, 1897.
—. "Girls Past and Present." *Ladies Home Journal* (Sept. 1920): 38, 141.
—. *Not Wisely but Too Well.* London: Tinsley Brothers, 1871.
Caird, Mona. *The Daughters of Danaus.* 1894. Rpt. New York: The Feminist P, 1989.
Casteras, Susan P. "Reader, Beware: Images of Victorian Women and Books." *Nineteenth-Century Gender Studies* 3.1 (Spring 2007): http://www.ncgsjournal.com/issue31/casteras.htm.
Cholmondeley, Mary. *Red Pottage.* 1899. Ed. Elaine Showalter. London: Penguin-Virago, 1985.
Debenham, Helen. "*Not Wisely But Too Well* and the Art of Sensation." *Victorian Identities: Social and Cultural Formations in Nineteenth-Century Literature.* Ed. Ruth Robbins and Julian Wolfreys. Hampshire: Macmillan; New York: St. Martin's, 1996. 9-24.
Fluhr, Nicole M. "Figuring the New Woman: Writers and Mothers in George Egerton's Early Stories." *Texas Studies in Literature and Language* 43.3 (Fall 2001): 243-66.
Gallagher, Catherine. "George Eliot and *Daniel Deronda*: The Prostitute and the Jewish Question." *Sex, Politics, and Science in the Nineteenth-

Century Novel. Ed. Ruth Bernard Yeazell. Baltimore: Johns Hopkins UP, 1986. 39-62.

Gilbert, Pamela K. *Disease, Desire and the Body in Victorian Women's Popular Novels.* Cambridge: Cambridge UP, 1997.

Gilbert, Sandra, and Susan Gubar. *The Madwoman in the Attic: The Nineteenth-Century Woman Writer and the Literary Imagination.* New Haven: Yale UP, 1979.

Hatten, Charles. *The End of Domesticity: Alienation from the Family in Dickens, Eliot, and James.* Unpublished manuscript, 2008.

Heller, Tamar. *Dead Secrets: Wilkie Collins and the Female Gothic.* New Haven: Yale UP, 1992.

—. "'That Muddy, Polluted Flood of Earthly Love': Ambivalence about the Body in Rhoda Broughton's *Not Wisely but Too Well.*" *Victorian Sensations: Essays on a Scandalous Genre.* Ed. Kimberly Harrison and Richard Fantina. Columbus: The Ohio State UP, 2006. 87-101.

—. Introduction. *Cometh Up as a Flower* xxxiii-l.

[James, Henry.] "An American and an English Novel." *The Nation* (21 Dec. 1876): 372-73.

Jones, Shirley. "'LOVE': Rhoda Broughton, writing and re-writing romance." *Popular Victorian Women Writers.* Ed. Kay Boardman and Shirley Jones. Manchester: Manchester UP, 2004. 208-36.

Leckie, Barbara. *Culture and Adultery: The Novel, the Newspaper, and the Law, 1857-1914.* Philadelphia: U of Pennsylvania P, 1999.

Ledger, Sally. *The New Woman: Fiction and Feminism at the Fin-de-Siècle.* Manchester: Manchester UP, 1997.

Matus, Jill. *Unstable Bodies: Victorian Representations of Sexuality and Maternity.* Manchester: Manchester UP, 1995.

Murphy, Patricia. "Disdained and Disempowered: the 'Inverted' New Woman in Rhoda Broughton's *Dear Faustina.*" *Tulsa Studies in Women's Literature* 19.1 (Spring 2000): 57-79.

Nead, Lynda. *Myths of Sexuality: Representations of Women in Victorian Britain.* Oxford: Blackwell, 1988.

Oliphant, Margaret. "Novels." *Blackwood's Edinburgh Magazine* 102 (Sept. 1867): 257-80.

Peterson, Linda. "Mary Cholmondeley (1859-1925) and Rhoda Broughton (1840-1920)." *Kindred Hands: Letters on Writing by British and American Women Authors, 1865-1935.* Ed. Jennifer Cognard-Black and Elizabeth MacLeod Walls. Iowa City: U of Iowa P, 2006. 107-119.

—. "The Role of Periodicals in the (Re)making of Mary Cholmondeley as New Woman Writer." *Media History* 7.1 (2001): 33-40.

Phelps, Elizabeth Stuart. *The Story of Avis*. 1877. Rpt. ed. Carol Farley Kessler. New Brunswick: Rutgers UP, 1985.

Pykett, Lyn. "Portraits of the Artist as a Young Woman: Representations of the Female Artist in the New Woman Fiction of the 1890s." *Victorian Women Writers and the Woman Question*. Ed. Nicola Diane Thompson. Cambridge: Cambridge UP, 1999. 135-50.

—. *The Improper Feminine: The Women's Sensation Novel and the New Woman Writing*. London: Routledge, 1992.

Review of *Not Wisely But Too Well* and *Cometh Up as a Flower*. *The Spectator* (19 Oct. 1867): 1172-74.

Sadleir, Michael. "Melodrama of the Breaking Heart." *Times Literary Supplement* (30 Nov. 1940): 604.

Wollstonecraft, Mary. *A Vindication of the Rights of Woman*. 1792. Ed. Carol Poston. 2nd ed. New York: Norton, 1988.

Wood, Marilyn. *Rhoda Broughton: Profile of a Novelist 1840-1920*. Stanford: Paul Watkins, 1993.

Woolf, Virginia. *A Room of One's Own*. 1929. New York: Harcourt Brace Jovanovich, 1957.

—. "Professions for Women." *Women and Writing*. Ed. Michèle Barrett. New York: Harcourt Brace Jovanovich, 1979. 57-63.

—. *To the Lighthouse*. 1927. New York: Harcourt Brace Jovanovich, 1955.

Notes

[1] For example, in an article on Mary Cholmondeley's *Red Pottage*, Ardis claims "I choose this novel as my representative[New Woman] text because it is about the New Woman novel" ("'Retreat with Honour,'" 334). See also Pykett, *The Improper Feminine* (177) and "Portraits of the Artist" for more on the popularity of the New Woman kunstlerroman. Ledger notes that "one of the striking features of many New Woman novels is that they are peopled with female writers of feminist fiction" (27).

[2] Indeed, Broughton's self-presentation as a well-bred lady rather than a serious artist informs Helen Black's account of an interview with her in *Notable Women Authors of the Day* (1893). Admittedly, being between novels at the time of Black's visit allowed Broughton to show her visitor a desk which contained "no indication of her work" but instead showcased "exquisitely painted" portfolios and china inkstands (40). Yet Broughton's erasure of her professional existence, replaced by references to her connoisseurship of genteel bric-a-brac, is not solely the consequence of her work schedule. Black declares that

No solitary copy can be seen, in the well-filled book-cases, of the author's works. She says that she sells them out at once, and then has "done with them"; but "Come," she adds, "we have talked long enough about my books: let me show you a few of my treasures[.] (44)

[3] See Leckie chapters 2 and 3, esp. 92-95.

[4] For more on journalistic and fictional representations of infanticide, see Matus, ch. 4, "Maternal Deviance" (157-212).

[5] For visual images of the trangressiveness of women's reading, see Casteras.

[6] For more on Broughton's use of intertextuality to bolster her literary authority and enable her revision of literary conventions, see Debenham and Heller, Introduction to *Cometh Up* xxxv-xxxvi. Flint also notes that Broughton's numerous allusions to reading foster an interpretive bond between author and reader (283-84).

[7] I have addressed the split between female-identified "low" fiction and male-identified "high fiction" that grew out of the late nineteenth-century professionalization of writing in *Dead Secrets* (see esp. 83-93). See also Hatten ch. 5 for more on Henry James's devaluation of female fiction. It is fascinating that Broughton was such good friends with James, notoriously hostile to women's writing and the high priest of the proto-modernist apotheosis of the serious (male) writer. Indeed, the two writers met soon after James's scathing review of Broughton's *Joan* (1876), which he likened to the "gambols of an elephant" in its "immaturity and crudity of art" (373). That James, like many of Broughton's contemporaries, prized her wit but apparently never discussed her work with her suggests, once again, how Broughton's fiction was valued less highly than her more "feminine" qualities as society *grande dame.*

[8] Char's situation also recalls the state of being "at strife against herself" that, in *A Room of One's Own,* Woolf identified as the inevitable fate of female intellectuals, such as her hypothetical "Judith Shakespeare," in the Elizabethan age: "Chastity had then, it has even now, a religious importance in a woman's life, and has so wrapped itself round with nerves and instincts that to cut it free and bring it to the light of day demands courage of the rarest. To have lived a free life in London in the sixteenth century would have meant for a woman was poet and playwright a nervous stress and dilemma which might well have killed her" (51-52).

[9] Wollstonecraft frequently criticizes discourses of romantic love for their sexual objectification of women, using the image of the seraglio, or harem, as a symbol of women's imprisonment in inegalitarian marriages; see, for example, pp. 29-31.

[10] For more on Broughton's Wollstonecraftian critique of marriage, see Heller, introduction to *Cometh Up as a Flower* xxxvii-xxxviii and "'That Muddy, Polluted Flood'" 92-96.

[11] In a novel whose central character aspires to emulate the author of *Jane Eyre* it is surely not coincidental that Mr. Delaval's first name is St. John, reminiscent of the chillingly oppressive clergyman who wishes to marry Jane in that novel.

CONTRIBUTORS

Tracy J.R. Collins teaches in the English Department at Central Michigan University. She has published articles and given talks on subjects from Joseph Conrad to the teaching of sports literature, and from Shaw to anti-feminist sentiments in baseball novels. She is currently working on a book length project that looks at the role of athletics and physical fitness in the emergence of the New Woman.

Casey Cothran is an adjunct professor at Winthrop University in Rock Hill, SC. Her publications focus on New Woman writers as well as the presentation of disability in the works of Victorian detective novelist Wilkie Collins.

Donna Decker is Associate Professor of English at Franklin Pierce University in Rindge, New Hampshire. She is also director of the Honors Program and the Women in Leadership Program. Decker received her doctorate at Northeastern University in Boston, her dissertation focusing on marriage in the New Woman novel.

Stacey Floyd is an Assistant Professor of English at Cardinal Stritch University in Milwaukee, Wisconsin. She is currently working on an essay for MLA's *Options for Teaching Laboring-Class Literature* and is co-editor of the journal *Nineteenth-Century Gender Studies*. Her research and teaching interests include representations of the working class in the long nineteenth century as well as women's writing and body studies.

Tamar Heller, associate professor of English and Comparative Literature at the University of Cincinnati, is author of *Dead Secrets: Wilkie Collins and the Female Gothic* (Yale UP, 1992), and of articles on such authors as the Brontës, J. S. Le Fanu, Margaret Oliphant, and Edith Wharton. She has also co-edited *Approaches to Teaching Gothic Fiction* (MLA: 2003) and *Scenes of the Apple: Food and the Female Body in Nineteenth- and Twentieth-Century Women's Writing* (SUNY, 2003). The editor of Rhoda Broughton's *Cometh Up as a Flower* for Pickering and Chatto's *Varieties of Women's Sensation Fiction* (2004), Professor Heller is currently at work on a book-length study of Broughton's fiction.

Kelly Hulander is an ABD Ph.D. candidate in English Literature at the University of Minnesota, Twin Cities. Her dissertation project is entitled, "'My life…will be employed in working for the people': Images of Community and Social Justice in British Women's New Woman and Socialist Fiction, 1880 – 1910." Hulander has been on the faculty of the College of Visual Arts in Saint Paul since 2004; she also serves on the Editorial Board of *Paj Ntaub Voice*, the first Hmong-American literary journal.

Abigail Mann is an ABD Ph.D. candidate at Indiana University, writing a dissertation entitled *Darwin's Sisters: Observational Experiments in Sisterhood in the Late Nineteenth-Century.* Her project seeks to understand exactly how Darwinism was deployed as a pro-female rights discourse at the end of the nineteenth century in both England and America. Examining the fiction of George Eliot, Mona Caird, and Charlotte Perkins Gilman, she traces their observational experimentation of potentialities, a methodology drawn from Darwinian ideas which focuses on the idea of creating and observing constant minute variations in conditions with the recognition that there are no fixed narratives, but multiple possibilities.

Melissa Purdue is an Assistant Professor at Minnesota State University-Mankato. Her research focuses on representations of motherhood, interracial marriage and women's sexuality in New Woman colonial fiction. She is currently editing an edition of Rosa Campbell Praed's *Fugitive Anne: A Romance of the Unexplored Bush* (1902) for Valancourt Books and is co-editor of the journal *Nineteenth-Century Gender Studies.*

Bryony Randall is currently a lecturer in English Literature at the University of Glamorgan. She will be joining the Department of English Literature at the University of Glasgow in September 2007. Her primary research interests lie in modernist literature, particularly the early modernist period. Her first book, *Modernism, Daily Time and Everyday Life* is forthcoming from Cambridge University Press (November 2007). She has also published on Imagist poetry, Gertrude Stein, and lifewriting, and is on the editorial board of the new journal *Pilgrimage: the journal of Dorothy Richardson studies.* She is currently working on a second major project provisionally entitled *The Working Woman Writer 1880-1920*, exploring the relationships between work, writing and gender in the early modernist period.